222 Homemade Mousse Recipes

(222 Homemade Mousse Recipes - Volume 1)

Jessica Adamson

Copyright: Published in the United States by Jessica Adamson/ © JESSICA ADAMSON

Published on October, 12 2020

All rights reserved. No part of this publication may be reproduced, stored in retrieval system, copied in any form or by any means, electronic, mechanical, photocopying, recording or otherwise transmitted without written permission from the publisher. Please do not participate in or encourage piracy of this material in any way. You must not circulate this book in any format. JESSICA ADAMSON does not control or direct users' actions and is not responsible for the information or content shared, harm and/or actions of the book readers.

In accordance with the U.S. Copyright Act of 1976, the scanning, uploading and electronic sharing of any part of this book without the permission of the publisher constitute unlawful piracy and theft of the author's intellectual property. If you would like to use material from the book (other than just simply for reviewing the book), prior permission must be obtained by contacting the author at author@bisquerecipes.com

Thank you for your support of the author's rights.

Content

222 AWESOME MOUSSE RECIPES 7

1. 3 Minute Chocolate Mousse Recipe 7
2. 60 Second Chocolate Mousse Recipe 7
3. Amaretto Mascarpone Creme Recipe 7
4. Avocado Chocolate Mousse Recipe 8
5. Bakers Mousse Bars Recipe 8
6. Banana Mousse Cake Recipe 9
7. Bitter Sweet Orange Clove Mousse Recipe 9
8. Bittersweet Chocolate Mousse Refrigerator Cake Recipe 10
9. Black Forest Cherry Mousse Recipe 10
10. Blackberry Mousse Recipe 11
11. Blue Mousse Recipe 11
12. Blueberry Mousse Recipe 11
13. Brave Chocolate Rum Mousse Recipe 12
14. Butter Pecan Mousse Recipe 12
15. Butterscotch Rum Mousse Recipe 12
16. CHEATS CARAMEL MOUSSE Recipe . 13
17. CHOCOLATE MOUSSE AU GRAND MARNIER Recipe 13
18. Cafe Mocha Mousse Recipe 13
19. Cantaloupe Mousse Recipe 14
20. Cappuccino Dessert Recipe 14
21. Cappuccino Mousse Recipe 15
22. Cate Olsens Chocolate Mousse Recipe 15
23. Cherry Cheesecake Mousse Recipe 15
24. Cherry Topped Chocolate And Cinnamon Mousse Recipe 16
25. Choccy Mud Mousse Recipe 16
26. Choco Burst Recipe 17
27. Choco Strawberry Mousse Puffs Recipe ... 17
28. Chocolate And Cinnamon Mousse Recipe 18
29. Chocolate And Cointreau Mousse Recipe 18
30. Chocolate And Marshmallows Mousse Recipe 19
31. Chocolate Kahlua Mousse Trifle Recipe... 19
32. Chocolate Marshmallow Mousse Recipe .. 19
33. Chocolate Meringue And Vanilla Mousse Recipe 20
34. Chocolate Mouss Recipe 20
35. Chocolate Mousse Cake Recipe 21
36. Chocolate Mousse Crepes Recipe 21
37. Chocolate Mousse Filled Crepes With Rich Cocoa Sauce Recipe 22
38. Chocolate Mousse In Chocolate Shells With Raspberry Sauce Recipe 22
39. Chocolate Mousse Napoleons Recipe 23
40. Chocolate Mousse Napoleons With Strawberries And Cream Recipe 24
41. Chocolate Mousse Pillow Recipe 24
42. Chocolate Mousse Recipe 25
43. Chocolate Mousse Torte Recipe 25
44. Chocolate Mousse In Chocolate Shells With Raspberry Sauce Recipe 26
45. Chocolate Orange Mousse Recipe 27
46. Chocolate Ricotta Mousse Recipe 27
47. Chocolate Ricotta Mousse With Raspberry Couli Recipe 27
48. Chocolate Silk & Peanut Butter Crunch Recipe 28
49. Chocolate Teacups Filled With Chocolate Mint Mousse Recipe 29
50. Chocolate Truffle Mousse Bars Recipe 30
51. Chocolate And Fig Mousse Recipe 30
52. Chocolate Mousse In Minutes Recipe 30
53. Chocolate Hazelnut Mousse Recipe 31
54. Citrus Mousse Cheesecake Recipe 31
55. Classic Chocolate Mousse Recipe 32
56. Cocoa Cappuccino Mousse Recipe 32
57. Cocoa Mousse Recipe 32
58. Coconut Mousse Recipe 33
59. Coffee Chocolate Mousse Via Delta Point River Restaurant Recipe 33
60. Cold Cherry Mousse With Vanilla Sauce Recipe 33
61. Comfort Mango Mousse Creamy Recipe .. 34
62. Cool Whip Chocolate Mousse Recipe 34
63. Cranberry Mousse Recipe 35
64. Cranberry Mousse With Chocolate Ganache Recipe 35
65. Cream From Heaven Natas Do Céu Recipe 36
66. Creamy Cappuccino Mousse Recipe 36
67. Creamy White Mousse With Fresh Raspberries Recipe 36
68. Creme Au Chocolat Glace Aka Rich Chocolate Mousse Recipe 37
69. Dark Chocolate Mousse Recipe 37
70. Dark Chocolate Mousse With Baileys And

- Mascarpone Cream Recipe 38
- 71. Deadly Dark Chocolate Mousse Recipe.... 38
- 72. Dessert Recipe 39
- 73. Disneys Jack Daniels Mousse Cake Recipe 39
- 74. Double Chocolate Velvet Mousse Recipe 40
- 75. Dutch Cocoa Mousse Slice With Ginger Bread Recipe Recipe 40
- 76. Easy Bittersweet Chocolate Mousse Cake Recipe 41
- 77. Easy Chocolate Mousse Recipe 42
- 78. Easy Double Chocolate Mousse Recipe ... 42
- 79. Easy Pumpkin Mousse Recipe 42
- 80. Easy Raspberry Iced Mousse Recipe 43
- 81. Easy Strawberry Mousse Recipe 43
- 82. Easy White Chocolate Mousse Recipe 43
- 83. Eggnog Mousse Recipe 44
- 84. Fake Out Mousse Recipe 44
- 85. French Vanilla Custard Mousse Recipe 44
- 86. Fresh Rasberry Mousse Recipe 45
- 87. Frozen Chocolate Mousse Squares Recipe 45
- 88. Frozen Mint Chocolate Mousse Recipe 45
- 89. Fudgy Peanut Butter Mousse Cups Recipe 46
- 90. Ganache / Mousse! Recipe............................ 46
- 91. German Chocolate Mousse Recipe............. 47
- 92. Ginger And Caramel Mousse Recipe 47
- 93. Grasshopper Mousse Recipe........................ 48
- 94. Graveyard Pumpkin Mousse Recipe.......... 48
- 95. Guinness Black And White Mousse Recipe 48
- 96. HAZELNUT MOUSSE Recipe 49
- 97. Harvest Mousse With Spiced Almond Tuiles Recipe 49
- 98. Hazelnut And Chocolate Mousse Recipe . 50
- 99. Hazelnut Chocolate Mousse Recipe Recipe 51
- 100. Hoochs Rich Chocolate Mousse Recipe... 51
- 101. Hybiscus Flower Gelatine With Lychee Mousse Recipe 51
- 102. Island Creams Recipe 52
- 103. Jello Chocolate Mousse Recipe.................... 52
- 104. Kahlua Mousse Recipe 53
- 105. Kamora Chocolate Mousse Recipe............. 53
- 106. Key Lime Mousse Cups Recipe 53
- 107. Key Lime Mousse Recipe 54
- 108. Key Lime Mousse With Jetts Gingersnap Cookies Recipe..54
- 109. Lemon Lime Mousse Recipe 55
- 110. Lemon Mascarpone Mousse Recipe 55
- 111. Lemon Mousse Cake Recipe 55
- 112. Lemon Mousse Recipe 56
- 113. Lemon Mousse With Fresh Berries Recipe 56
- 114. Lemon Mousse With Fresh Berries Recipe 57
- 115. Lemon And Cocoa Mousse Recipe............58
- 116. Lemon And White Chocolate Mousse Parfaits With Strawberries Recipe.....................58
- 117. Light Chocolate Mousse Recipe 59
- 118. Light Strawberry Mousse Recipe 59
- 119. Lime Mango Mousse In Chocolate Cups Recipe..59
- 120. Lime Mousse Recipe 60
- 121. Low Fat Dark Chocolate Mousse Recipe .60
- 122. Low Fat Oreo Mousse Recipe......................60
- 123. Lusciously Rich Chocolate Pie Recipe.......61
- 124. Mango Berry And Lemon Mousse Dessert Recipe..61
- 125. Mango Mousse Recipe...................................62
- 126. Mango And Orange Mousse Recipe 62
- 127. Maple Nut Mousse Pie Recipe 62
- 128. Midnight Mousse Recipe...............................63
- 129. Milk Chocolate Coffee Mousse In A Cocoa Nib Florentina Cup Recipe 63
- 130. Mimi's Chocolate Mousse Recipe................64
- 131. Mocha Marshmallow Mousse Recipe 65
- 132. Mocha Tortoni MOUSSE Recipe 65
- 133. Mom's Cherry Cheesecake Recipe..............65
- 134. Mothers Day Chocolate Mousse With Sauce Recipe..66
- 135. Mothers Day Nutella Mousse Recipe 66
- 136. Mousse Berry Shells Recipe 67
- 137. Mousse Chocolat With A Dash Of Cinnamon And Rum Recipe..............................67
- 138. Mousse Chocolate Tart Recipe 68
- 139. Mousse Chokolat Recipe...............................68
- 140. Mousse Au Chocolat Recipe 68
- 141. My Chocolate Mousse Recipe 69
- 142. No Cook Faux Chocolate Or Cinnamon Or Cappuccino Mousse Recipe..............................69
- 143. No Bake Nutella Cheesecake Recipe 70
- 144. Nutella Mousse Recipe 70
- 145. ORANGE CHOCOLATE MOUSSE

Recipe 71
146. OREO CHOCOLATE MOUSSE Recipe 71
147. Orange And Almond Mousse Recipe 71
148. Oreo Cookie Desert Recipe 72
149. Oreo Mousse Recipe 72
150. Party Size Chocolate Cherry Mousse Recipe 72
151. Passion Fruit Mousse Recipe 73
152. Passionfruit And White Chocolate Mousse Recipe 73
153. Peach Mousse Recipe 74
154. Peanut Butter Mousse Cake Recipe 74
155. Pear Mousse Recipe 74
156. Pears With Chocolate Mousse And White Sauce Recipe 75
157. Pecan And Chocolate Mousse Twinkie Dessert Recipe 75
158. Pineapple Mousse Recipe 76
159. Prune Mousse Recipe 76
160. Pumpkin Mousse 77
161. Pumpkin Mousse Parfait Recipe 77
162. Pumpkin Mousse Recipe 78
163. Pumpkin Mousse In Cinnamon Pastry Shells Recipe 78
164. Pumpkin Pudding Whip Recipe 78
165. Quick And Easy Chocolate Mousse Recipe 79
166. Quick Mousse L'orange Recipe 79
167. Quick And Easy Chocolate Mousse Recipe 79
168. Raspberry And Chocolate Yogurt Desert Recipe 80
169. Raspberry Mousse Recipe 80
170. Raspberry White Chocolate Mousse Recipe 81
171. Red Raspberry Mousse Recipe 81
172. Rich Chocolate Mousse Recipe 81
173. Ricotta Mousse With Berries Recipe 82
174. Simple Chocolate Mousse Recipe 82
175. Simple Strawberry Mousse Recipe 82
176. Simply Chocolate Mousse Recipe 83
177. Slow Cooker Chocolate Mocha Mousse Recipe 83
178. Square Deals Recipe 83
179. Strawberry Jello Mousse Recipe 84
180. Strawberry Margarita Mousse Recipe 84
181. Strawberry Mousse Parfait Recipe 85

182. Strawberry Mousse Recipe 86
183. Strawberry Mousse Squares Recipe 86
184. Strawberry Mousse Torte Recipe 86
185. Super Duper Easy Chocolate Mousse Recipe 87
186. Swiss Chocolate Mousse Torte Recipe 87
187. Szechuan Pepper Chocolate Mousse Recipe 88
188. Tequila Mousse With Raspberry Sauce Recipe 88
189. Three Chocolate Mousse Cake Recipe 89
190. Tofu Chocolate Mousse Recipe 90
191. Tofunana Cream Recipe 90
192. Triple Chocolate Overload Mousse Cake Recipe 90
193. Triple Chocolate Mousse Cake Recipe 92
194. Triple Chocolate Mousse Cake Recipe 93
195. Two Whiskey Chocolate Mousse Recipe .. 94
196. Utah Strawberry Chocolate Mousse Recipe 95
197. Valentine Parfait White Chocolate Mousse With Red Raspberry Coulis Recipe 95
198. Valentines Day Chocolate Mousse Recipe 96
199. WISCONSIN MASCARPONE MOUSSE WITH HAZELNUT DESSERT Recipe 96
200. Whisky Mousse Recipe 97
201. White Chocolate Coconut Mousse Recipe 97
202. White Chocolate Lime Mousse Recipe 97
203. White Chocolate Mousse 98
204. White Chocolate Mousse In Milk Chocolate Shells Recipe 98
205. White Chocolate Mousse Recipe 99
206. White Chocolate Mousse Tarts Recipe 99
207. White Chocolate Mousse With Fresh Raspberry Sauce Recipe 99
208. White Chocolate Mousse With Raspberry Swirl Recipe 100
209. White Chocolate Mousse With Strawberries Recipe 101
210. White Chocolate Raspberry Mousse Recipe 101
211. White Chocolate Grand Marnier Mousse In Chocolate Pistachio Tuile Cups Recipe 102
212. White Milk And Dark Chocolate Mousse Recipe 102
213. White Chocolate Mousse Recipe 103
214. Wildly Chocolate Brownies With Mousse

Topping Recipe 104
215. Wills Chocolate Mousse Recipe 104
216. Yogurt Mousse Recipe 105
217. Brownie White Chocolate Mousse Torte Recipe 106
218. Chocolate Marshmallow Mousse Recipe 106
219. Chocolate Hazelnut Mousse Recipe 107
220. Lemon And White Chocolate Mousse Parfaits With Strawberrys Recipe 107
221. Mint Caramel Mousse Recipe 108
222. Passion Fruit Mousse Recipe 108

INDEX 109
CONCLUSION 111

222 Awesome Mousse Recipes

***

1. 3 Minute Chocolate Mousse Recipe

Serving: 4 | Prep: | Cook: 60mins | Ready in:

Ingredients

- 6 ounces chocolate chips or more expensive bittersweet chocolate broken into pieces.
- 1 egg
- 1 teaspoon vanilla
- 2 teaspoons Grand Marnier liqueur or cognac
- 4 teaspoons sugar
- 3/4 cup whole milk
- pinch of salt

Direction

- Place chocolate, egg, vanilla, Grand Marnier or Cognac, sugar and a pinch of salt into a blender and blend just enough to mix.
- Heat milk until just about to boiling.
- Pour milk into blender and blend for 1 more minute.
- Pour into 4 dessert cps and refrigerate for an hour.
- SAVOR THE FLAVOR.
- Just note, the quality of the chocolate does affect the taste. More expensive chocolate is enhanced by the liqueur.

2. 60 Second Chocolate Mousse Recipe

Serving: 4 | Prep: | Cook: 5mins | Ready in:

Ingredients

- 1 c. chocolate chips
- 1 c. heavy cream
- 1 egg
- 1 tsp. vanilla or liqueur to flavor
- whipped cream

Direction

- Place chocolate, egg and flavouring in blender or food processor and chop. Heat cream until small bubbles appear at edge. Do not boil. With machine running, pour in hot cream. Blend until chocolate is melted and mixture is smooth. Pour into dessert dishes and cover with plastic and chill. Serve with whipped cream on top.
- Could even use mint chocolate chips, raspberry chocolate chips, Andes candies bits, etc. etc. etc.
- Mel's note: Made this for Christmas Dinner and for a party. It is WONDERFUL! - December 2006

3. Amaretto Mascarpone Creme Recipe

Serving: 6 | Prep: | Cook: 10mins | Ready in:

Ingredients

- 500 g (about 2 cups) mascarpone cheese
- 250 g (about 1 cup) heavy whipping cream
- 1/4 cup powdered sugar
- 3 TBS amaretto liqueur
- 1 cup Italian Amaretto biscuits (cookies), crushed

Direction

- Crush the amaretto biscuits in a large Ziploc bag with a rolling pin until finely crumbled, but not to powder.
- In a large mixing bowl, combine the Mascarpone, whipping cream, sugar and Amaretto.
- Beat on low speed until combined and then on high speed until very thick.
- In a glass bowl, layer crumbs and cream, finishing with a few crumbs on top for decoration.
- Chill well, at least 3 hours, before serving.
- Can also be frozen; in that case, remove from freezer 15 minutes before serving.

4. Avocado Chocolate Mousse Recipe

Serving: 4 | Prep: | Cook: 25mins | Ready in:

Ingredients

- 1 1/2 medium avocado
- 4 sections chocolate, 100% Cacao, chopped
- 4 tsp Honey Raw
- 1 tsp coconut Oil

Direction

- Bring a small pan with about 1-inch of water to a boil.
- Turn the heat off, and put a bowl on top, as a lid.
- Place the chopped chocolate in the bowl, so it melts with the steam from the water underneath it.
- Mix with a spatula every now and then until it is completely melted.
- Transfer the melted chocolate to a blender or food processor, together with the avocado, honey, and coconut oil.
- Process until completely smooth (make sure there are no avocado pieces left).
- Pour the mixture into 4 shot glasses, and refrigerate for an hour or longer.
- Optional: Before serving, garnish each portion with a sliced strawberry and/or a mint leaf.
- =
- Nutrition Facts
- Serving Size: 1 servings
- Amount per Serving
- Calories 188
- Calories from Fat 147.2
- % Daily Value *
- Total Fat 16.35g
- 24%
- Saturated Fat 6.02g
- 30%
- Cholesterol 3.33mg
- 1%
- Sodium 4.27mg
- 0%
- Total Carbohydrate 15.25g
- 7%
- Dietary Fibre 6.75g
- 26%
- Sugars 5.35g
- Protein 2.79g
- 1%
- Est. Percent of Calories from:
- Fat
- 37%
- Carbs
- 32%
- Protein
- 5%
- * Percent Daily Values are based on a 2,000 calorie diet. Your daily values may be higher or lower depending on your calories needs.

5. Bakers Mousse Bars Recipe

Serving: 18 | Prep: | Cook: 25mins | Ready in:

Ingredients

- 1 pkg. (8 squares) BAKER'S Semi-sweet chocolate, divided
- 1/2 cup sugar
- 1/4 cup flour
- 1 can (14 oz.) EAGLE BRAND® sweetened condensed milk, divided
- 4 eggs
- 1 pkg. (3.9 oz.) JELL-O chocolate instant pudding
- 1-1/2 cups thawed Cool Whip whipped topping

Direction

- HEAT oven to 325°F.
- MELT 6 chocolate squares as directed on package. Mix with sugar, flour, 1/4 cup condensed milk and eggs until well blended. Pour into 9-inch square pan sprayed with cooking spray.
- BAKE 25 min. or until toothpick inserted in center comes out clean. (Do not overbake.) Cool completely.
- BEAT dry pudding mix and remaining condensed milk with whisk 2 min. Stir in COOL WHIP; spread over dessert. Melt remaining chocolate squares; drizzle over pudding layer. Refrigerate until chocolate is firm.

6. Banana Mousse Cake Recipe

Serving: 12 | Prep: | Cook: 180mins | Ready in:

Ingredients

- Sponge cake
- 125g caster sugar
- 4 eggs
- 1/2tablespoon cake emulsifier
- 100 superfine flour
- 1teaspoon vanilla essence
- 45ml water
- 65g corn oil or melted butter
- banana Mousse

- (A)
- 4000g mashed potato
- 1/2g lemon(squeezed the juice out)
- 1/8banana essence
- (B)
- 11/2 tablespoon gelatin powder
- 25ml water
- (C)
- 200g non daily whipping cream
- 21/2tablespoon icing sugar
- For garnish
- 150g non daily whipping cream
- 1 banana thinly slice

Direction

- To make sponge cake
- Beat all ingredients (corn oil not included) until fluffy and in oil and mix well.
- Pour batter into a lined a greased 20 square tin and bake for 108 Celsius for 35 to 45 minutes until cooked, remove and cool on a rack.
- Banana Mouse
- Double boil all ingredient (B) until dissolved Beat (C) till stiff, (A) and (B) mix well.
- Slice sponge cake into to 2 pieces in side way and place one piece in the 20cm loose base square tin. Pour banana mousse on the top and cover with another piece of the sponge cake and chill for 2 to 3 hours
- Whisk non-daily whipping cream until stiff, spread on the mousse cake and placed the thinly sliced banana one over lapping the other on top
- Be sure to cut the banana last so that it won't oxidize.

7. Bitter Sweet Orange Clove Mousse Recipe

Serving: 4 | Prep: | Cook: 360mins | Ready in:

Ingredients

- .5 cups sugar

- 2 tbsp butter
- ½ - ¾ tsp cloves, powdered
- 1 orange, zest
- 2 sheets of gelatine
- The oranges, juiced
- 1 cup fresh cream

Direction

- Set your gelatine sheets in water to soak.
- Melt sugar and butter in a small pan.
- Add in orange zest and juice, and clove powder and bring to a boil.
- Filter this liquid mix, then put the gelatine in. Stir until dissolved and let it cool while stirring occasionally.
- Now whip up your cream until stiff and then once the above liquid is cooled mix together. This needs to be entirely blended before you put the mousse into bowls.
- Leave to sit in refrigerator for 3-4 hours.
- Now serve with some chocolate shavings on top!

8. Bittersweet Chocolate Mousse Refrigerator Cake Recipe

Serving: 0 | Prep: | Cook: 8hours30mins | Ready in:

Ingredients

- 2 cups chilled heavy cream
- one 10-ounce jar bittersweet chocolate sauce (1 cup plus 2 tablespoons)
- one 9-ounce package chocolate wafers
- Shaved bittersweet chocolate, for garnish

Direction

- 1. In a large chilled stainless steel or glass bowl, using a handheld electric mixer, beat the heavy cream with the chocolate sauce at medium speed until firm peaks form. Spread about 1/2 cup of the whipped chocolate cream on a long rectangular platter to form a 3-by-10-inch rectangle.
- 2. Using a small offset spatula, spread 1 tablespoon of the remaining chocolate cream on 35 chocolate wafers and arrange them in 5 stacks. Top each stack with a chocolate wafer (you will have 6 or 7 wafers left over). Arrange the wafer stacks on their sides as close together as possible on the chocolate cream on the platter. (The wafer stacks will lie lengthwise on the platter.) Spread all but about 1/2 cup of the remaining chocolate cream all over the cake, fixing any wafers that tilt or slide.
- 3. Press a long sheet of plastic wrap over the cake, flattening the top and sides gently. Refrigerate for at least 8 hours or for up to 2 days. Refrigerate the remaining chocolate cream.
- $.Discard the plastic wrap and frost the cake with the remaining chocolate cream, smoothing the top and sides. Garnish with the chocolate shavings. Cut into slices, wiping the knife after each cut.

9. Black Forest Cherry Mousse Recipe

Serving: 8 | Prep: | Cook: | Ready in:

Ingredients

- 2 cups milk
- 1 package (3.9 ounces) instant chocolate pudding mix
- 1 can (21 ounces) cherry pie filling
- 2 cups whipped topping

Direction

- In a bowl, beat the milk and pudding mix for 2 minutes or until smooth.
- Let stand until slightly thickened, about 2 minutes.
- Stir in pie filling.

- Gently fold in whipped topping.
- Spoon into individual dessert dishes; refrigerate until serving.
- Top with chocolate shavings, maraschino cherry etc.

10. Blackberry Mousse Recipe

Serving: 4 | Prep: | Cook: 5mins | Ready in:

Ingredients

- 1 cup blackberry juice with no pulp or seeds
- 1 envelope unflavored gelatin
- 1 teaspoon fresh lemon juice
- 1 cup granulated sugar
- 1 cup whipping cream
- 1 teaspoon vanilla
- 1 graham cracker pie crust

Direction

- In a saucepan combine blackberry juice and lemon juice then sprinkle gelatine over juice. Bring to a slow boil stirring constantly. Once slow boil is maintained add sugar. Cook and stir about one minute to dissolve sugar thoroughly. Pour into a bowl and refrigerate until it becomes syrupy but not set. Whip cream and vanilla to soft peak stage. Gently pour cream into blackberry gelatine mixture. Fold and stir gently until an even colour is achieved. Pour into graham cracker crust then refrigerate or freeze.

11. Blue Mousse Recipe

Serving: 0 | Prep: | Cook: 90mins | Ready in:

Ingredients

- 8oz cream cheese, softened
- 3/4 cup powdered sugar, divided
- juice from 1/2 lemon
- 2-3T natural fruit spread(I used this Blueberry Jam) .. you can use any any flavor, but, then the title of the recipe will change. ;)
- 2 cups heavy whipping cream
- 1t vanilla
- fresh berries for serving, optional

Direction

- In bowl of electric mixer, beat cream cheese with 1/2 cup powdered sugar until fluffy and smooth.
- Add lemon juice and fruit spread and beat well.
- Remove to a large bowl and set aside.
- Rinse bowl, ending with COLD water, then hand dry with clean towel or paper towels (you don't want the bowl warm)
- Now beat whipping cream with vanilla, and remaining 1/4 cup of sugar at high speed until stiff peaks form.
- Add about 1/2 of the whipped cream mixture to the cream cheese mixture, and hand stir until well combined. You don't have to be gentle with this.
- Add remaining whipped cream mixture and GENTLY fold until combined.
- Refrigerate covered in large bowl or in individual serving bowls, for at least 1 hour.

12. Blueberry Mousse Recipe

Serving: 0 | Prep: | Cook: 5mins | Ready in:

Ingredients

- 1 pint fresh clean blueberries
- 1/4 cup sugar
- 1 cup heavy cream
- 1 cup mascarpone cheese
- 1 tsp vanilla

Direction

- Place blueberries then cream, vanilla and mascarpone cheese in a high speed blender
- Pulse till thick (only a few seconds)
- Serve immediately or chill (mixture with thicken with standing) but this is best when freshly made.
- Note: Don't over pulse as the cream may get too firm an actually become clumpy

13. Brave Chocolate Rum Mousse Recipe

Serving: 4 | Prep: | Cook: 5mins | Ready in:

Ingredients

- 1/4 cup granulated sugar
- 4 tablespoons rum
- 1/4 pound semisweet chocolate melted over double boiler
- 2 egg whites
- 2 cups whipped cream

Direction

- Combine sugar and rum then stir into melted chocolate until smooth.
- When mixture is cool but not chilled fold into it stiffly beaten egg whites then gently fold in whipped cream.
- Chill in sherbet glasses at least 2 hours before serving.

14. Butter Pecan Mousse Recipe

Serving: 4 | Prep: | Cook: 5mins | Ready in:

Ingredients

- 3/4 cup pecan pieces
- 1 tablespoon butter melted
- 16 ounces cream cheese softened
- 1/4 cup granulated sugar
- 1/4 cup firmly packed brown sugar
- 1/2 teaspoon vanilla extract
- 1 cup whipping cream whipped

Direction

- Combine pecans and butter stirring well then spread on a baking sheet.
- Bake at 350 for 5 minutes then finely chop nuts and set aside.
- Beat cream cheese at medium speed with an electric mixer until smooth.
- Add sugars and vanilla beating well then stir in 3/4 cup toasted pecans.
- Gently fold whipped cream into pecan mixture and spoon or pipe into serving dishes.
- Garnish with additional nuts if desired.

15. Butterscotch Rum Mousse Recipe

Serving: 4 | Prep: | Cook: 120mins | Ready in:

Ingredients

- 2/3 c. butterscotch pieces
- 2 tblsp. dark rum
- 3 large egg yolks
- 1/4 c. sugar
- a few drops of maple flavoring
- 4 large egg whites
- dash of salt
- dash of cream of tartar
- 3/4 c. whipping cream(not whipped)
- for garnish
- toasted slivered almonds
- mint leaves are pretty too

Direction

- Melt the butterscotch in a small pan, in a large pan of hot, not boiling, water
- Mix in the rum, let cool

- Beat egg yolks, add sugar and maple flavouring, and combine with the butterscotch/rum mixture
- Beat egg whites until foamy
- Add the dashes of salt and cream of tartar, beat until firm (not stiff) peaks appear
- Beat a little of the egg white into the butterscotch mix to loosen,
- Gently fold the butterscotch mixture into the egg whites
- Whip the cream into soft peak stage
- Fold into butterscotch mixture
- Divide evenly into 4 or 6 small dishes
- Chill 2 hours
- Garnish with whipped cream, slivered almonds, mint

16. CHEATS CARAMEL MOUSSE Recipe

Serving: 4 | Prep: | Cook: 2mins | Ready in:

Ingredients

- 1Tablespoon milk
- 3 x 62.5g Mars Bars, thinly sliced
- 300 ml (1/2 pint) double cream, lightly whipped.
- whipped cream , to decorate.
- Bag of Maltesers.

Direction

- Put the milk and Mars Bars together in a heatproof bowl. Melt over hot water or in the microwave on full power for about 2 minutes, stirring half way through, until smooth and completely melted.
- Set aside to cool a little.
- Mix a couple of tablespoons of the whipped cream into the caramel mixture and fold in the remaining whipped cream and spoon into 4 x size 1 ramekins or glasses.
- Transfer to the fridge to set for about an hour for a soft set or overnight for a firmer set.
- Decorate with a blob of cream and sliced or whole Maltesers.

17. CHOCOLATE MOUSSE AU GRAND MARNIER Recipe

Serving: 6 | Prep: | Cook: 5mins | Ready in:

Ingredients

- 1 (4-ounce) package sweet baking chocolate
- 4 (1-ounce) squares semisweet chocolate
- 1/4 cup Grand Marnier or other orange-flavored liqueur
- 2 cups whipping cream
- 1/2 cup sifted powdered sugar
- Garnishes: orange rind strips, whipped cream

Direction

- Combine first 3 ingredients in top of a double boiler; bring water to a boil.
- Reduce heat to low; cook until chocolates melt.
- Remove from heat, and cool to lukewarm.
- (Mixture will thicken and appear grainy as it cools.)
- Beat whipping cream until foamy; gradually add powdered sugar, beating until soft peaks form.
- Gently fold about one-fourth of whipped cream mixture into chocolate mixture; fold in remaining whipped cream mixture.
- Spoon into individual dishes; chill until ready to serve.
- Garnish, if desired.

18. Cafe Mocha Mousse Recipe

Serving: 12 | Prep: | Cook: 1mins | Ready in:

Ingredients

- CAFÉ MOCHA

- 1/3 cup heavy whipping cream
- 1 tablespoon cold water
- 1/2 teaspoon plain gelatin
- 3 tablespoons powdered sugar
- 1/4 teaspoon instant coffee powder
- 2 tablespoons semisweet chocolate chips
- 15 Athens® Mini Fillo Shells (1 box)
- 2 tablespoons shredded coconut, for garnish
- Optional: 1 tablespoon Kahlua

Direction

- In a small chilled bowl, whip heavy cream to full volume.
- Chill for 1 hour.
- In a small pan, combine water, Kahlua and gelatine and let stand for 1 minute.
- Add powdered sugar, instant coffee and chocolate chips.
- Over low heat stir until chocolate chips are melted.
- Bring to room temperature.
- Gently fold the chocolate mixture into the whipped cream.
- Chill for 1 hour.
- Spoon or pipe 2 teaspoons of filling into each Fillo Shell.
- Garnish with shredded coconut. Serve immediately.
- Tip: When the mousse has set, just put it all into large baggie, pushing it down to one corner of the bag and twist the top, squeezing the mousse tightly into that corner. With scissors, cut a small hole and squeeze the mousse directly into either the phyllo cups, on top of cupcakes, into small bowls or on to cake or into a cooked and cooled pie shell.

19. Cantaloupe Mousse Recipe

Serving: 8 | Prep: | Cook: | Ready in:

Ingredients

- Note: You will need a very nice ripe cantaloupe for this recipe.
- 2 Tablespoons (2 packages) unflavored gelatin
- 1/3 Cup apricot (or) orange juice
- 1/4 Cup Curacao (a) orange liqueur
- 1 about 2-1/2 or 3 Pound Ripe cantaloupe, peeled and chunked
- 3 Tablespoons sugar
- 2 Tablespoons lemon juice
- 1/3 Cup plain yogurt

Direction

- Place the gelatine in a small saucepan, and pour in the Juice and let set a few minutes to soften.
- Add the Curacao and stir over low heat until the gelatine is completely dissolved.
- In a blender or food processor, puree the melon with the sugar and lemon juice.
- Pour in the gelatine mixture through the feed tube while the motor is running.
- Blend in the yogurt.
- Spoon the mousse into a bowl and refrigerate several hours or overnight, until well set.
- Serve in sherbet glasses.

20. Cappuccino Dessert Recipe

Serving: 0 | Prep: | Cook: 10mins | Ready in:

Ingredients

- 1 packet (1.5ounce) Jell-O Vanilla flavor Fat Free Sugar Free Instant Pudding
- 2 teaspoons Maxwell House instant coffee, or to your taste
- 2 cups cold fat free milk
- 1/8 teaspoon ground cinnamon
- 1 cup thawed Cool Whip lite whipped topping

Direction

- 1. Beat dry pudding mix, coffee granules and milk with whisk for about 2 minutes.

- 2. Pour into 5 dessert dishes.
- 3. Refrigerate for 1 hour.
- 4. Stir cinnamon into cool whip with whisk and spoon over pudding.

21. Cappuccino Mousse Recipe

Serving: 4 | Prep: | Cook: 180mins | Ready in:

Ingredients

- 1 envelope unflavored gelatin
- ½ cup hot water
- 2/3 cup instant nonfat milk powder
- 2 tsp instant espresso powder
- 1 tbsp unsweetened cocoa
- 2 tsp brown sugar
- pinch salt
- 1/2 cup ice water

Direction

- In a blender container, sprinkle gelatine over water and let stand to soften about 5 minutes.
- Process until dissolved.
- Add remaining ingredients except ice water and blend smooth.
- With motor running, add cold water. The mixture should begin to thicken and froth.
- Chill 1 hour.
- Using blender or electric beaters, whip until aerated.
- Portion into 4 coffee cups (or bowls). Cover and chill again for 1-2 hours.

22. Cate Olsens Chocolate Mousse Recipe

Serving: 6 | Prep: | Cook: | Ready in:

Ingredients

- 1/3 cup brewed coffee, very hot
- 6 ounces chocolate chips
- 4 egg yolks
- 2 tablespoons Kahlua
- 4 egg whites

Direction

- Combine coffee and chips in food processor until melted. Add yolks, liqueur and process until thick and smooth. Beat whites until stiff. Pour chocolate mixture over whites and fold in until no white streaks remain. Spoon into wine glasses and chill at least one hour.
- Top with sweetened whipped cream with a little added Kahlua. Recipe may be doubled.

23. Cherry Cheesecake Mousse Recipe

Serving: 10 | Prep: | Cook: | Ready in:

Ingredients

- 1 pound fresh or frozen pitted sweet cherries
- 1-1/2 teaspoons unflavored gelatin
- 1 package (8 ounces) cream cheese, softened
- 1/2 cup confectioners' sugar
- 4 squares (1 ounce each) while baking chocolate, melted
- 2 teaspoons vanilla extract
- 1 cup heavy whipping cream

Direction

- Place the cherries in a food processor or blender; cover and process until chopped. Transfer to a saucepan; stir in the gelatine. Let stand for 1 minute.
- Bring to a boil; reduce heat. Cook and stir for 1 minute or until the gelatine is dissolved. Transfer to a bowl. Refrigerate for 45 minutes or until the mixture begins to thicken.
- In a small mixing bowl, beat cream cheese until smooth. Beat in the confectioners' sugar,

chocolate and vanilla until combined. Fold in cherry mixture. In another mixing bowl, beat whipping cream until soft peaks form. Fold into the cherry cream mixture. Pour into dessert dishes. Cover and refrigerate for 3 hours or until set.

24. Cherry Topped Chocolate And Cinnamon Mousse Recipe

Serving: 4 | Prep: | Cook: 10mins | Ready in:

Ingredients

- For the cherry topping:
- 8 ounces fresh bing cherries, pitted
- 1/3 cup black cherry preserves or other cherry preserves
- 1/3 cup ruby port or cherry juice
- For the Mousse
- 1 1/4 cups chilled heavy whipping cream, divided
- 1/8 teaspoon (generous) ground cinnamon
- 4 ounces bittersweet or semisweet chocolate, chopped
- Extra whipped cream for garnish

Direction

- For cherries:
- Combine cherries, cherry preserves, and Port in heavy small saucepan. Bring to boil over high heat. Reduce heat to medium and boil until juices thicken to syrup consistency, stirring frequently, about 10 minutes. Remove from heat. Transfer to small bowl and chill until cold, about 3 hours.
- DO AHEAD Can be made 1 day ahead. Cover and keep chilled.
- For mousse:
- Combine 1/4 cup cream and cinnamon in small saucepan; bring to boil. Remove from heat. Add chocolate and whisk until melted and smooth. Transfer chocolate mixture to large bowl. Using electric mixer, beat remaining 1 cup cream in medium bowl until soft peaks form. Fold 1/4 of whipped cream into lukewarm chocolate mixture. Fold remaining whipped cream into chocolate mixture in 3 additions just until incorporated. Divide mousse among 4 glasses or bowls. Chill until set, about 4 hours.
- When serving, divide the cherry topping among the 4 glasses, on top of the mousse, garnish with some more whipped cream.
- I arranged a tiny chocolate-cherry cookie on top of each glass. Chocolate-cherry cookie.

25. Choccy Mud Mousse Recipe

Serving: 610 | Prep: | Cook: 3mins | Ready in:

Ingredients

- 300 ml cream
- 250 g dark chocolate chips, melts or chocolate bits
- 3 egg yolks (the whites can be stored in a small covered container in the fridge for 2 – 3 weeks. Great for pavlova. Remember 1 egg white = approximately 50 ml)
- 2 tablespoons caster sugar

Direction

- Pour the cream into a microwave proof jug or bowl and cook on high for 2 – 3 minutes until just about to boil, watch carefully so it doesn't overflow.
- Place the chocolate, egg yolks and caster sugar in a blender, pour in the nearly boiling cream. Securely fit on the lid and blend until smooth and well combined. This will take about 30 seconds.
- Pour into serving dishes or small glasses. This mousse looks really good in tiny coffee cups or fancy little glasses. Set in the fridge for at least 3 hours.

- Serve with a dollop of whipped cream and some chopped chocolate or pieces of fruit. Keeps well for 3 – 4 days in the fridge.

26. Choco Burst Recipe

Serving: 0 | Prep: | Cook: 1hours | Ready in:

Ingredients

- dark chocolate - H/F PACK
- WHITE CHOCOLATE- H/F PACK
- FLAVORED cake - 2 PIECES
- strawberry jelly - 25 GM
- whipped cream -100 GM
- GRATED WHITE CHOCLATE
- TUTY-FRUITY
- nuts
- vanilla ice-CREAM

Direction

- 1. MELT BOTH WHITE AND DARK CHOCOLATE AND KEEP IT ASIDE FOR FEW MINUTES.
- 2. TAKE YOUR FLAVORED CAKE AND CUT IT INTO SMALL CUBES.
- 3. WHIP ICE-CREAM
- 4. NOW, TAKE ANY TYPE OF SERVING DISH [BOWL, GLASS, CONTAINER, ETC], IT'S BETTER IF YOU USE TRANSPARENT GLASS.
- 5. PUT SOME JELLY IN GLASS AND SPREAD IT THOROUGHLY IN GLASS, ADD SOME TUTY-FRUITY.
- 6. ADD SOME CAKE CUBES, WHIPPED CREAM, AGAIN SOME CAKE CUBES, MELTED WHITE CHOCOLATE.
- 7. AT LAST ADD 1 SCOOP OF VANILLA ICE-CREAM AND DARK CHOCOLATE.
- 8. PUT FEW NUTS ON IT.
- 9. AND SERVE CHILLED.

27. Choco Strawberry Mousse Puffs Recipe

Serving: 6 | Prep: | Cook: 30mins | Ready in:

Ingredients

- Pastry~
- 1/2 cup (1 stick) butter
- 1 cup water
- 1/2 teaspoon salt
- 4 eggs, room temp (i put mine in a bowl with very warm water, much faster)
- 1 cup flour
- ~Mousse~
- 1 1/2 cups hulled strawberries, hulled (measure after running through food processor. (it's about 2 cups whole)
- 1 pkg strawberry flavored gelatin
- 1 pint whipping cream, whipped
- ~Topping~
- 3 oz melted chcoclate

Direction

- Bring butter and water to a boil in medium saucepan.
- Add flour in all at once and stir until it begins to pull away from sides and forms a ball in the centre of saucepan.
- Let cool for 5 minutes.
- Beat eggs in one at a time until smooth.
- Drop on well-greased baking sheet a couple of inches apart, you can either make long or small éclairs or big or small puffs, your choice.
- Bake in a preheated 400 degree oven for 30 minutes or until golden brown. Do not over bake!!!
- Remove to cooling rack and cool till you can handle, slice open with a serrated knife and remove dough in middle, allow to dry 30 minutes to 1 hour before filling.
- Bring strawberries to a boil in a saucepan, remove from heat and add the gelatine. Pour into a bowl and let sit till almost set. Carefully fold in whipped cream, refrigerate.

- When mousse is set and puffs are completely cool, fill each puff with mixture and drizzle with melted chocolate. (I melted 3 oz. of semi-sweet in the microwave, slowly)

28. Chocolate And Cinnamon Mousse Recipe

Serving: 4 | Prep: | Cook: | Ready in:

Ingredients

- 8 ounces dark chocolate, grated or crushed
- 1 cup whipping cream
- 1/2 teaspoon powdered cinnamon
- 1 tablespoon unsweetened cocoa powder

Direction

- Place grated chocolate in bowl. Pour 1/3 of whipping cream in a small pan and cook on low heat almost to a boil. Remove from heat. Add chocolate and cinnamon; blend gently and well. Set aside.
- In an electric mixer, add the remaining whipping cream until firm consistency. Incorporate the chocolate mixture using a wooden spoon. Add cocoa; blend gently and well. Refrigerate the mousse for several hours. (* There isn't a cooking time included in this recipe. Just heat chocolate almost to a boil)

29. Chocolate And Cointreau Mousse Recipe

Serving: 8 | Prep: | Cook: | Ready in:

Ingredients

- ~chocolate Mousse~
- 12 oz Semisweet dark chocolate
- 6 egg whites
- 1/4 Cup superfine sugar...caster
- 2 teaspoons gelatin...dissolved in 2 tablespoons boiling water
- 2 1/3 Cups Heavy double cream,softly whipped
- ~ Cointreau Mousse~
- 4 egg yolks
- 1/4 Cup superfine sugar
- 1/4 Cup Freshly Squeezed orange juice
- 2 teaspoon Geltin
- 1/4 Cup Cointreau
- 2 Cup heavy double cream,softly whipped
- 4 orange,in segments.
- Grated chocolate

Direction

- ~Chocolate Mousse~
- Melt the chocolate, stir occasionally, until melted.
- Set aside to cool.
- Beat egg whites until soft peaks form.
- Scrape the chocolate into a bowl.
- Carefully stir in the dissolved gelatine into the melted chocolate.
- Then alternately fold in the whipped cream and the egg whites until well combined.
- Set aside until ready to use.
- ~ Cointreau~
- Beat the egg yolks and sugar until pale and creamy.
- Bring half the orange juice to a boil, remove from heat, and add gelatine.
- Stir until completely dissolved.
- Stir in the remaining orange juice and liqueur.
- Gradually whisk the gelatine mixture into the egg yolks and sugar.
- Fold in the cream.
- Spoon Chocolate Mousse into piping bag fitted with a star nozzle.
- Set out 8 long stemmed glasses on a tray.
- Place some of the orange segments in the base of each glass.
- Pipe in generous rosettes of the chocolate mousse.
- Top with more orange segments and more chocolate mousse.

- Finish with a few more segment and a large dollop of the Cointreau mousse.
- Decorate with grated chocolate.
- Chill in the refrigerator for 30 minutes before serving
- ~ Nice Chilled Dessert ~

30. Chocolate And Marshmallows Mousse Recipe

Serving: 8 | Prep: | Cook: 30mins | Ready in:

Ingredients

- 18 oz good quality dark chocolate, mininum 60% cocoa solids, chopped
- 10 Oz mini marshmallows (or normal size marshmallows cut in half)
- 3 oz unsalted butter
- 1/2 cup recently boiled water
- 3 1/2 cups double cream

Direction

- In a heavy sauce pan melt chocolate, marshmallows, butter and water. Stir until you get a silky chocolate paste.
- Set aside to cool.
- Whip the cream until you get firm peaks. Fold onto the chocolate paste.
- Put in individual ramekins or in a large bowl.
- Put the mousse in the fridge for 30 minutes to 1 hour and it is ready to serve!

31. Chocolate Kahlua Mousse Trifle Recipe

Serving: 10 | Prep: | Cook: 30mins | Ready in:

Ingredients

- 1 box chocolate cake mix
- 1 cup Kahlua
- 4 small boxes chocolate mousse instant pudding
- 4 toffee candy bars
- 16 ounces frozen whipped topping thawed

Direction

- Prepare cake according to package then let cake cool and pierce with a fork several times.
- Drizzle Kahlua into holes then chill overnight in pan.
- Break up cake and place half in a glass trifle bowl.
- Prepare pudding according to package directions.
- Add a layer of pudding, 2 crushed candy bars and a layer of whipped topping.
- Add remaining cake and repeat the layer process.
- Top with frozen whipped topping and remaining crushed candy bars.

32. Chocolate Marshmallow Mousse Recipe

Serving: 6 | Prep: | Cook: 20mins | Ready in:

Ingredients

- 1 pkg of white marshamallows, 10 oz
- 6 oz of semi sweet chocolate (squares or quality chips)
- 1 cup heavy cream
- 6 lady fingers (storebought)
- butterscoth schnapps as needed
- butterscoth chips
- 6 marachino cherries
- whipped cream

Direction

- Melt marshmallows on lowest heat stirring constantly.

- If mixture sticks, pour in a little heavy cream to make melting easier.
- Melt chocolate and stir smooth.
- Whisk chocolate into marshmallow mixture till loose and smooth.
- Let cool a bit
- Whip the cream and blend into mixture.
- Into 6 (or more) dessert glasses, add some mouse, break up one lady finger and place over mousse, drizzle some schnapps and cover with more mousse.
- Sprinkle on chips over top.
- Repeat with each dessert
- Chill well
- Before serving, spritz top of each dessert with whipped cream and top with a cherry

33. Chocolate Meringue And Vanilla Mousse Recipe

Serving: 6 | Prep: | Cook: 3mins | Ready in:

Ingredients

- For the chocolate meringue:
- 100 g powder sugar
- 15 g cocoa powder
- 4 egg whites
- 100 g sugar
- For the vanilla mousse:
- 4 egg yolks
- 50 g sugar
- 250 ml milk
- 250 ml cream
- 1 teaspoon vanilla extract
- 1 vanilla pod
- 3 gelatine sheets

Direction

- For the meringue preheat oven to 120°C.
- Sift powder sugar and cocoa powder together.
- Beat egg whites stiff and add half of the sugar while beating.
- Fold in the rest of the sugar, after whisk in the powder sugar-cocoa mixture.
- Pipe meringue on a baking sheet and bake for 30 minutes with a partly open oven (use a wooden spoon to keep it open). Reduce temperature to 100°C and bake it for 1 more hour. Shut the oven down and let the meringue dry for 2 more hours by a half opened oven.
- For the mousse warm milk, sugar, vanilla extract, vanilla pod and bring it boil.
- Whisk it to the egg yolks and let it thicken while whisking over steam.
- Whisk in gelatine sheets (that you soaked in water before) and let it cool.
- Stir in beaten cream and leave it in the fridge for 2-3 hours before serving.

34. Chocolate Mouss Recipe

Serving: 6 | Prep: | Cook: 10mins | Ready in:

Ingredients

- chocolate 100 grams
- butter 50 gram
- eggs 3
- milk ¼ cup
- Coco powder 1 tbsp
- sugar 75 gram
- vanilla essence ½ tsp
- gelatin 1 tsp
- water ¼ cup
- fresh cream 200 grams
- caster sugar 1 cup

Direction

- Melt chocolate over pan of boiling water. Add butter, milk, coco powder and mix well
- Now beat eggs with caster sugar very well till they turn fluffy.
- Then add vanilla essence.
- Fold the chocolate mixture into the egg mixture and add gelatine very gradually.

- Then fold in the whipped cream Chill till firm or set
- Decorate with fresh cream and chocolate decorations

35. Chocolate Mousse Cake Recipe

Serving: 4 | Prep: | Cook: 60mins | Ready in:

Ingredients

- 500g dark chocolate
- 2 tablespoons golden syrup
- 125g unsalted butter
- 4 eggs
- 1 tablespoon caster sugar
- 1 tablespoon plain flour, sifted
- Melted chocolate, to decorate
- chocolate ice cream, to serve

Direction

- 1. Preheat oven to 220°C. Grease and line the base of a 20cm round spring-form cake pan with non-stick baking paper.
- 2. Melt the chocolate, golden syrup and butter in a bowl over a saucepan of gently simmering water. Set aside to cool slightly.
- 3. Place eggs and sugar in a bowl. Using an electric mixer, beat on high for 10 minutes until very thick and pale. Gently fold in the flour then fold in the chocolate mixture until combined. Pour into the cake pan and bake on the middle shelf of the oven for 12 minutes. Remove from oven and run a knife around the edge of the cake. Remove collar from cake pan and transfer the cake to the fridge for 1 hour to cool.

36. Chocolate Mousse Crepes Recipe

Serving: 8 | Prep: | Cook: 15mins | Ready in:

Ingredients

- Crepes:
- 1-1/2 cups flour
- 1 tablespoon sugar
- 1/4 teaspoon salt
- 2 cups milk
- 1 teaspoon vanilla
- 3 eggs
- 2 tablespoons butter melted
- vegetable oil
- 8 eggs
- 12 ounce package semi-sweet chocolate chips
- 4 tablespoon rum
- 1 cup granulated sugar

Direction

- Combine flour, sugar, salt, milk and vanilla beating until smooth.
- Add eggs and beat well then stir in butter. Refrigerate batter at least 2 hours. Cook crepes on crepe pan or in skillet with oil.
- Pour 2 tablespoons batter into pan. Quickly tilt pan in all directions so batter covers pan in a thin film. Cook 1 minute or until lightly brown.
- Take 3 bowls. Separate eggs placing egg yolks in a bowl, four whites in second bowl and remaining four whites in third bowl. Melt chocolate over low heat then add yolks 1 at a time beating well after each addition. Blend in rum. Remove from heat and cool slightly.
- Beat 4 egg whites in each bowl until frothy. Gradually add 1/2 cup sugar to each bowl and beat until stiff peaks form. Stir small amount of whites into chocolate mixture. Combine whites and gently fold chocolate mixture. Refrigerate filling at least one hour then fill crepes and top with dollop of whipped cream and a few sliced almonds before serving.

37. Chocolate Mousse Filled Crepes With Rich Cocoa Sauce Recipe

Serving: 8 | Prep: | Cook: 20mins | Ready in:

Ingredients

- 2 eggs beaten
- 1-1/2 cups milk
- 1 cup all purpose flour
- 2 tablespoons granulated sugar
- 1 tablespoon cooking oil
- 1/4 teaspoon salt
- Mousse:
- 1 teaspoon unflavored gelatin
- 1 tablespoon cold water
- 2 tablespoons boiling water
- 1/2 cup granulated sugar
- 1/2 cup unsweetened cocoa powder
- 1 cup whipping cream
- 1 teaspoon vanilla
- Sauce:
- 1 cup granulated sugar
- 1/3 cup unsweetened cocoa powder
- 2 tablespoons cornstarch
- 2/3 cup evaporated milk
- 1 tablespoon butter

Direction

- To make crepes combine eggs, milk, flour, sugar, cooking oil and salt then beat until mixed.
- Heat a lightly greased crepe pan and remove from heat.
- Spoon in 2 tablespoons batter and tilt pan to spread batter.
- Return to heat and brown one side only then invert over paper towels to remove crepe.
- Repeat greasing pan as needed.
- For mousse in small mixing bowl sprinkle gelatine over cold water and let stand 1 minute.
- Add boiling water then stir until gelatine is completely dissolved then cool.
- In large mixing bowl stir together sugar and cocoa powder then add whipping cream and vanilla.
- Beat with electric mixer on low speed until thickened scraping bowl occasionally.
- Add gelatine and stir until well mixed then cover and chill 30 minutes.
- Fold each crepe in half then spread 1-1/2 tablespoons mousse onto each folded crepe.
- Fold crepe again then drizzle sauce over top and serve immediately.
- For sauce in small saucepan combine sugar, cocoa and cornstarch.
- Gradually add evaporated milk and butter then cook until bubbly then cook 1 minute more.
- Stir in vanilla and serve warm over crepes.

38. Chocolate Mousse In Chocolate Shells With Raspberry Sauce Recipe

Serving: 9 | Prep: | Cook: 10mins | Ready in:

Ingredients

- 2 pounds bittersweet chocolate broken into pieces
- 8 tablespoons unsalted butter
- 2/3 cup coffee
- 2/3 cup Kahlua
- 4 egg yolks
- 8 egg whites at room temperature
- 8 tablespoons granulated sugar
- 2 cups heavy cream
- chocolate Shells:
- scallop shells or like sized shallow dishes
- 3/4 pound bittersweet chocolate
- Raspberry Sauce:
- 4 pints fresh raspberries
- 4 cups sugar
- 2 tablespoons cornstarch
- fresh raspberries for garnish

Direction

- Melt chocolate, butter and coffee in top of double boiler over simmering water stir occasionally.
- In small bowl whisk Kahlua into egg yolks.
- Remove double boiler from heat and gradually whisk Kahlua egg yolk mixture into chocolate.
- Set aside to cool to room temperature.
- In a separate large bowl beat egg whites with an electric mixer on low speed until foamy.
- Turn speed to high and beat until soft peaks form.
- Beat sugar a little at a time into egg whites and spoon over chocolate mixture but do not fold in.
- Beat cream in the same mixing bowl with mixer on low speed until thicken.
- Beat on medium speed until soft peaks form.
- Fold chocolate mixture with egg whites into cream.
- Cover with plastic wrap and refrigerate 4-6 hours.
- To make shells cover back of scallop shells with aluminum foil.
- Melt chocolate in a microwave or double boiler.
- Paint chocolate onto foil with a pastry brush (leave small space around edge of shell).
- Put shells into freezer until firm.
- Separate shell from chocolate and foil.
- Peel foil off chocolate leaving a nice chocolate shell that needs to be kept refrigerated until used.
- To make sauce puree raspberries in a saucepan then add sugar and bring to a boil.
- Thicken with a mixture of cornstarch and water (2 tablespoons cornstarch in 1/2 cup water).
- Put one scoop of mousse onto each chocolate shell then top with raspberry sauce.
- Garnish with fresh raspberries.

39. Chocolate Mousse Napoleons Recipe

Serving: 18 | Prep: | Cook: 90mins | Ready in:

Ingredients

- 1/2 of a 17.3 ounce-package Pepperidge Farm® puff pastry sheets (1 sheet), thawed
- 1 cup heavy cream
- 1/4 teaspoon ground cinnamon
- 1 package (6 ounces) semi-sweet chocolate pieces, melted and cooled (about 1 cup)
- 1 square (1 ounce) semi-sweet chocolate, melted
- confectioners' sugar

Direction

- Heat the oven to 400°F.
- Unfold the pastry sheet on a lightly floured surface. Cut the pastry into 3 strips along the fold marks. Cut each strip into 6 rectangles. Place the pastries 2-inches apart on 2 baking sheets.
- Bake the pastries for 15 minutes or until they're golden brown. Remove the pastries from the baking sheets and cool on a wire rack for 10 minutes.
- Put the cream and cinnamon in a medium bowl. Beat with an electric mixer set on high speed until stiff peaks form. Fold in the melted chocolate pieces. Split each pastry into 2 layers, making 36 pieces. Spread 18 bottom halves with the chocolate cream mixture. Top with the remaining top halves. Serve immediately or cover and refrigerate up to 4 hours.
- Drizzle the pastries with the chocolate and sprinkle with confectioners' sugar just before serving.
- TIP Easy Substitution: You can substitute 2 cups thawed frozen non-dairy or dairy whipped topping for the heavy cream.

40. Chocolate Mousse Napoleons With Strawberries And Cream Recipe

Serving: 12 | Prep: | Cook: 15mins | Ready in:

Ingredients

- 1/2 package Pepperidge Farm frozen puff pastry Sheet
- 1 cup heavy cream
- 1/2 tsp. cinnamon
- 1 cup semi-sweet chocolate pieces, melted and cooled
- (I use bittersweet chocolate chips.)
- 1/2 cup bittersweet chocolate melted and cooled
- 2 cups whipped topping or sweetened whipped cream (see below)
- 1 1/2 cups sliced strawberries (bananas are great, too!)
- Optional: powdered sugar for dusting finished napoleon
- *Sweetened cream recipe: 1 cup of heavy cream, 2 TB of sugar,
- and 1/2 tsp. vanilla extract. Whip this all together until stiff. This makes 2 cups of cream!
- Alternative dessert options:
- Use bananas, blueberries (fresh not frozen), mangos and follow the recipe as shown.
- You can use a vanilla mousse, too! Add one small box of instant vanilla pudding to 2 cups of whole milk and beat until firm. I use the sugar-free instant pudding and its great! Use this instead of the chocolate mousse. You can actually fold this into one cup of heavy cream that has been whipped for a "moussier" texture.

Direction

- Thaw the pastry sheet at room temperature for 30 minutes.
- Preheat your oven to 400 degrees.
- Unfold the pastry sheet and cut along the three fold marks into 3 long strips.
- Cut each strip into six small rectangles.
- Place each rectangle on to a baking sheet.
- Bake for 15 minutes until golden brown and let cool on a rack.
- ...
- Beat the cream and cinnamon in mixer until stiff. Fold in the 1 cup of melted and cooled chocolate.
- ...
- With a good knife, slip the blade between each pastry and split into two layers. Don't squeeze the pastry or it will crumble. Be gentle!
- ...
- Separate your layers of pastry into three groups of 12 layers each.
- Spread the chocolate cream or mousse layer on one layer,
- Top each one with another layer of pastry.
- Then top with the plain whipped cream or sweetened cream and then add a layer of strawberries.
- Top with another layer of pastry.
- Using the 1/2 cup of melted chocolate, drizzle the last layer of pastry with the chocolate lightly making strips or a design if you wish.
- You can now sprinkle with powdered sugar if you wish.

41. Chocolate Mousse Pillow Recipe

Serving: 16 | Prep: | Cook: 25mins | Ready in:

Ingredients

- 1 package of silken tofu
- 3/4 c. semisweet chocolate chips melted
- 1/4 c. maple syrup
- 1 tsp. vanilla extract
- 1/2 package of Nasoya wonton wrappers
- spray vegetable oil
- power sugar for topping
- chocolate syrup for topping, drizzle
- assorted fruits

- ice cream

Direction

- Put tofu in food processor and blend until completely smooth, about 2 minutes. Add melted chocolate chips, maple syrup, and vanilla extract, process until well blended, refrigerate for at least 2 hours.
- Spray a wonton wrapper with vegetable oil. Place 1 teaspoon filling in centre of wrapper. Moisten edges with water, fold into a triangle shape and then press to seal. Repeat. Place on a baking sheet that has been sprayed with oil.
- Lightly spray tops of filled wonton wrappers with oil and bake in 375°F oven for 10 to 12 minutes or until lightly browned.
- Garnish with powder sugar and drizzle with melted chocolate if desired. Serve with fruit and ice cream. Enjoy!!!

42. Chocolate Mousse Recipe

Serving: 4 | Prep: | Cook: | Ready in:

Ingredients

- chocolate Mousse:
- 4 ounces high quality bittersweet or semisweet chocolate, cut into small pieces
- 2 tablespoons unsalted butter, cut in small pieces
- 2 large eggs, separated
- 1/8 teaspoon cream of tartar
- 3 tablespoons sugar, divided
- 1/2 teaspoon pure vanilla extract
- 1/2 cup heavy whipping cream
- Garnish: (optional)
- whipped cream
- Fresh berries
- Shaved chocolate

Direction

- In a medium-sized stainless steel bowl set over a saucepan of simmering water, melt the chocolate and butter. Remove from heat and set aside to cool for a few minutes. Then whisk in the two egg yolks. Refrigerate.
- In the bowl of your electric mixer (or with a hand mixer), whip the two egg whites with the cream of tartar until foamy. Gradually add two tablespoons of sugar and continue to beat until stiff peaks form, yet the whites are still glossy and not dry. Set aside.
- In another bowl, whip the heavy cream, remaining one tablespoon sugar, and vanilla extract until soft peaks form.
- Remove the chocolate mixture from the refrigerator, and stir a couple of spoonfuls of the beaten egg whites into the chocolate mixture to lighten it, and then fold the remaining whites into the chocolate mixture, gently but thoroughly. Fold in the whipped cream.
- Spoon the chocolate mousse into four individual serving dishes or glasses. Cover and refrigerate for a couple of hours. Can serve with additional whipped cream, fresh berries and/or shaved chocolate.

43. Chocolate Mousse Torte Recipe

Serving: 8 | Prep: | Cook: 30mins | Ready in:

Ingredients

- 1 package one layer devils food cake mix
- 1/3 cup chocolate ice cream topping
- 4 squares semisweet chocolate
- 2 tablespoons powdered sugar
- 2 tablespoons coffee liqueur
- 2 egg yolks
- 1/2 cup whipped cream
- 1 tablespoon chocolate ice cream topping
- 1/2 cup whipped cream
- 1 cup fresh raspberries

Direction

- Prepare cake mix and bake according to directions then cool 10 minutes.
- Remove from pan and cool completely then place on serving platter.
- Spread cake with 1/3 cup ice cream topping and chill until needed then set aside.
- In a small saucepan melt semisweet chocolate over low heat then remove.
- Stir in powdered sugar, liqueur and egg yolks.
- Cook and stir over medium heat for 2 minutes or until mixture coats a metal spoon.
- Remove from heat and cool completely.
- Beat the first 1/2 cup whipping cream to soft peaks.
- Stir half of the chocolate mixture into the whipped cream then fold in the remaining chocolate.
- Cover and chill until mixture mounds.
- Spread onto cake to within 1 inch of edge then chill covered for several hours.
- To serve drizzle cake with 1 tablespoon topping.
- Using a pastry bag fitted with the star tip pipe the 1/2 cup whipped cream around cake edge.
- Garnish with raspberries.

44. Chocolate Mousse In Chocolate Shells With Raspberry Sauce Recipe

Serving: 6 | Prep: | Cook: 20mins | Ready in:

Ingredients

- 2 pounds bittersweet chocolate broken into pieces
- 8 tablespoons unsalted butter
- 2/3 cup coffee
- 2/3 cup Kahlua
- 4 egg yolks
- 8 egg whites at room temperature
- 8 tablespoons granulated sugar
- 2 cups heavy cream
- chocolate Shells:
- scallop shells or like sized shallow dishes
- 3/4 pound bittersweet chocolate
- Raspberry Sauce:
- 4 pints fresh raspberries
- 4 cups sugar
- 2 tablespoons cornstarch
- fresh raspberries for garnish

Direction

- Melt chocolate, butter and coffee in top of double boiler over simmering water stir occasionally.
- In small bowl whisk Kahlua into egg yolks.
- Remove double boiler from heat and gradually whisk Kahlua egg yolk mixture into chocolate.
- Set aside to cool to room temperature.
- In a separate large bowl beat egg whites with an electric mixer on low speed until foamy.
- Turn speed to high and beat until soft peaks form.
- Beat sugar a little at a time into egg whites and spoon over chocolate mixture but do not fold in.
- Beat cream in the same mixing bowl with mixer on low speed until thicken.
- Beat on medium speed until soft peaks form.
- Fold chocolate mixture with egg whites into cream.
- Cover with plastic wrap and refrigerate 4-6 hours.
- To make shells cover back of scallop shells with aluminum foil.
- Melt chocolate in a microwave or double boiler.
- Paint chocolate onto foil with a pastry brush (leave small space around edge of shell).
- Put shells into freezer until firm.
- Separate shell from chocolate and foil.
- Peel foil off chocolate leaving a nice chocolate shell that needs to be kept refrigerated until used.
- To make sauce puree raspberries in a saucepan then add sugar and bring to a boil.
- Thicken with a mixture of cornstarch and water 2 tablespoons cornstarch in 1/2 cup water).

- Put one scoop of mousse onto each chocolate shell then top with raspberry sauce.
- Garnish with fresh raspberries.

45. Chocolate Orange Mousse Recipe

Serving: 4 | Prep: | Cook: 10mins | Ready in:

Ingredients

- 6 squares semisweet chocolate
- 1 teaspoon grated orange rind
- 1/4 cup firmly packed brown sugar
- 2 egg yolks
- 2 eggs
- 1 tablespoon orange juice
- 1 cup whipping cream whipped
- mandarin oranges

Direction

- Melt chocolate over hot water in top of double boiler then cool.
- Combine orange rind, sugar, egg yolks and eggs in blender then blend until light and foamy.
- Add chocolate and orange juice then blend well and fold in whipped cream.
- Pour into small individual serving dishes then chill until set.
- Garnish each with additional whipped cream and mandarin orange slices.

46. Chocolate Ricotta Mousse Recipe

Serving: 6 | Prep: | Cook: 1hours | Ready in:

Ingredients

- 3 oz unsweetened chocolate, melted
- 1 pound ricotta cheese
- 1 tsp vanilla
- 1/3 cup honey

Direction

- Blend melted chocolate, cheese, vanilla and honey in blender until smooth.
- Pour into desert cups or glasses and chill.

47. Chocolate Ricotta Mousse With Raspberry Couli Recipe

Serving: 6 | Prep: | Cook: 30mins | Ready in:

Ingredients

- Couli:
- 2 cups fresh raspberries
- 3 tablespoons sugar
- juice of a lemon
- Mousse:
- unsalted butter, for greasing ramekins
- 6 ounces bittersweet chocolate (not unsweetened), chopped
- 1½ pounds fresh whole milk ricotta cheese, drained for 2 hours to remove excess liquid
- ¼ cup plus ⅓ cup sugar
- 3 large egg yolks
- 1 teaspoon orange zest
- ½ teaspoon pure almond extract
- ¼ teaspoon ground cinnamon
- ⅛ teaspoon salt
- 3 large egg whites
- ¼ teaspoon cream of tartar

Direction

- To make the coulis:
- Blend the berries, juice, and sugar in a food processor until smooth.
- Strain the puree through a fine mesh strainer or chinoise.
- Cover and refrigerate. (Can be made 8 hours ahead. Keep refrigerated.)

- To make the mouse:
- Preheat the oven to 325 degrees F.
- Lightly butter 6 (6-ounce) ramekins.
- Arrange the ramekins in a large roasting pan.
- Whisk the chocolate until it melts in a medium bowl set over a saucepan of simmering water. (Don't let the water actually boil, and don't ever let the bottom of the bowl touch the surface of the water.)
- Set the melted chocolate aside.
- Blend the ricotta, ¼ cup of sugar, egg yolks, orange zest, almond extract, cinnamon, and salt in a food processor until very smooth.
- Blend in the melted chocolate.
- Transfer the ricotta-chocolate mixture to a large bowl.
- Using an electric or stand mixer with the whisk attachment, beat the egg whites in another large bowl with the cream of tartar until soft peaks form.
- Gradually beat in the remaining ⅓ cup of sugar.
- Continue beating until semi-firm peaks form.
- Stir a couple of tablespoons of the egg whites into the ricotta-chocolate mixture, then fold in the rest.
- Spoon the mixture into the prepared ramekins.
- Fill the pan with enough hot water to come halfway up the sides of the ramekins.
- Bake until the mousse puffs slightly but the centres are still creamy, about 25 minutes (they will thicken as they cool).
- Allow the ramekins to cool slightly before removing from water bath.
- Cover and refrigerate until cold, about 3 hours.
- Run a knife around the side of a mousse to loosen. Invert it onto a plate.
- Drizzle the raspberry coulis around the mousse and serve. (Or you can put the coulis into a squeeze bottle and draw stripes across the plate before setting down the mousse.

48. Chocolate Silk & Peanut Butter Crunch Recipe

Serving: 12 | Prep: | Cook: 1hours | Ready in:

Ingredients

- 1 sleeve Ritz crackers, reduced fat
- 4 tbsp. melted butter
- 4 c. milk
- 4 eggs
- 1/2 c. sugar
- 5 tbsp. cornstarch
- 1/4 tsp. salt
- 1 tbsp. vanilla
- 1 c. powdered sugar
- 1 c. chunky peanut butter
- 1/2 c. coarsely chopped peanuts
- 1/2 sleeve Ritz crackers, reduced fat
- 1 c. butter, room temperature
- 1 1/2 c. sugar
- 6 tbsp. unsweetened cocoa
- 1 tsp. vanilla
- 4 eggs
- Mini peanut butter and Ritz crackers
- white chocolate

Direction

- Crush crackers very fine; add melted butter and press into 9" x 13" glass baking pan. Bake at 400° for 10 minutes or until lightly browned.
- Heat milk in saucepan. Blend eggs, sugar, cornstarch, and salt. When milk is hot, temper egg mixture with it before adding entire egg mixture to milk. Stir constantly until cooked through and thickened. Add vanilla. Pour over Ritz crust while both are still hot- it will prevent the crust from getting soggy. Cool with plastic wrap directly against vanilla custard to prevent skin from forming. Not all of the filling may be needed. You will want a 1/4" layer.
- Make crumbles with powdered sugar, peanut butter, peanuts, and crackers. Sprinkle generously over vanilla layer.

- Kitchen Aid works best for the French Silk. Whip butter; gradually add sugar until light and fluffy. Mix in cocoa and vanilla. Add two eggs and beat on high for five minutes. Scrape down sides of bowl, add two more eggs and beat five more minutes. Watch measurements and time carefully for this part or it will break down. Spoon on top of peanut butter crumbles.
- Dip mini peanut butter Ritz's in melted white chocolate and use for garnish. Thoroughly chill dessert and serve chilled.

49. Chocolate Teacups Filled With Chocolate Mint Mousse Recipe

Serving: 8 | Prep: | Cook: | Ready in:

Ingredients

- 8 cups (5-ounce bathroom size)
- 12 ounces semisweet chocolate, chopped
- mint Mousse:
- 3 cups heavy cream
- 12 ounces white baking chocolate, chopped
- 6 tablespoons white or green crème de menthe liqueur
- Garnish (optional):
- 1 candy cane, crushed

Direction

- 1. Teacups: Using scissors, on each cup cut 4 slits, evenly spaced, from top to bottom. Tape slits closed with masking tape on outside of cups
- 2. Place chopped chocolate in medium-size microwave-safe bowl. Microwave on high power for 1-1/2 minutes. Stir; microwave another 30 to 60 seconds or until almost melted. Stir to melt completely. Let stand about 1 minute or until temperature is about 115 degrees F on instant-read thermometer.
- 3. Place 2 heaping tablespoons melted chocolate in one cup. Swirl to coat inside of cup; use pastry brush to evenly coat. Place cup, open side up, on waxed paper-lined baking sheet. Working quickly, repeat with remaining 7 cups.
- 4. After 5 minutes, re brush chocolate evenly in cups. Place on waxed paper, open side down. Refrigerate while continuing.
- 5. Handles and Stirrers: Place remaining melted chocolate in small resealable plastic food-storage bag. Snip very small hole in one corner. On another waxed paper-lined baking sheet, pipe 8 handles in shape of letter D, about 1 inch high. For stirrers, on waxed paper, pipe 8 lines about 1-1/2 inches long and about 1/4 inch thick. (Make extra handles and stirrers to allow for breakage.) Refrigerate 15 minutes or until chocolate is firm. Reserve chocolate-filled plastic bag at room temperature.
- 6. Assemble Teacups: Remove masking tape from cup. Carefully peel cup away from chocolate. Gently pop bottom of chocolate cup from the paper cup. Repeat process.
- 7. Microwave reserved chocolate in plastic bag at 30 second intervals or until just melted. Pipe a 1-inch-long vertical line on side of cup. Using toothpick, gently lift a handle off waxed paper and place on melted chocolate to attach to cup. Repeat with remaining cups. Refrigerate 15 minutes until chocolate is firm, or up to a few days. (Reserve chocolate in plastic bag at room temperature for any repairs.)
- 8. Mint Mousse: In small saucepan, heat 3/4 cup heavy cream until small bubbles appear around edge of pan. Place chopped chocolate in large bowl. Pour hot cream over; let stand 1 minute. Stir until chocolate is melted. Stir in liqueur. Let cool 10 to 15 minutes or until mixture registers 80 degrees F on instant-read thermometer.
- 9. In large bowl, beat remaining heavy cream on medium-high speed until stiff peaks form. With whisk, stir about one-quarter of whipped cream into chocolate mixture to lighten. Gently fold in remaining whipped cream. Cover; refrigerate at least 2 hours or overnight.

- 10. To serve: Spoon mousse into large pastry bag fitted with large star tip; pipe into cups. (Cups can be filled 3 hours ahead; refrigerate.) Garnish with stirrers, and candy, if desired.
- Makes 8 cups.

50. Chocolate Truffle Mousse Bars Recipe

Serving: 8 | Prep: | Cook: 20mins | Ready in:

Ingredients

- pkg. (6 squares) BAKER'S SELECT Semi-sweet chocolate, divided
- 1/4 cup whipping cream
- 2 eggs
- 1/4 cup sugar
- 2 Tbsp. flour
- 1-1/2 cups thawed Cool Whip whipped topping

Direction

- HEAT oven to 325°F. Line 8-inch sq. pan with greased foil. Microwave 3 chocolate squares and cream in microwaveable bowl on HIGH 1 min. Whisk until chocolate is completely melted; cool. Add eggs, sugar and flour; mix well. Pour into pan.
- BAKE 20 min. or until toothpick inserted in center comes out clean. Cool. Meanwhile, melt 2 chocolate squares as directed on package; cool.
- STIR COOL WHIP into melted chocolate; spread onto dessert. Refrigerate 1 hour. Use ends of foil to lift dessert from pan. Cut into bars. Melt remaining chocolate square; drizzle over bars.

51. Chocolate And Fig Mousse Recipe

Serving: 4 | Prep: | Cook: | Ready in:

Ingredients

- 7 fresh figs, use whatever type you like best
- 1/2 pint vanilla Gelato (if necessary, use French vanilla ice cream)
- 2 tablespoons unsweetened cocoa powder
- 1/4 cup dark chocolate, shaved

Direction

- Set 1 fig aside for garnish, and peel the rest.
- In a food processor, combine the peeled figs, gelato (or ice cream) and cocoa powder. Puree until smooth.
- Transfer to serving dishes.
- Sprinkle with the shaved chocolate.
- Cut the reserved fig into quarters, the long way, and use 1/4 to garnish each serving dish.

52. Chocolate Mousse In Minutes Recipe

Serving: 6 | Prep: | Cook: 15mins | Ready in:

Ingredients

- 300g good-quality dark chocolate, roughly chopped
- 3 eggs
- 1/4 cup (55g) caster sugar
- 1 tbs good-quality cocoa powder, sifted
- 300ml thickened cream, plus extra whipped cream to serve
- Grated chocolate, to serve

Direction

- Place the chocolate in a heatproof bowl over a pan of gently simmering water (don't let the bowl touch the water). Stir until melted.

- Remove bowl from heat and set aside to cool slightly.
- Place eggs and sugar in a large bowl and beat with electric beaters for 5 minutes, or until mixture is pale, thick and doubled in volume. Fold in cooled chocolate and cocoa powder until combined.
- In a separate bowl, whip cream until thickened (be careful not to over-beat). Use a large metal spoon to carefully fold the cream into the chocolate mixture, trying to keep the mixture as light as possible. Spoon into 6 serving glasses and chill in fridge for at least 1 hour. Remove from fridge 15 minutes before serving, then top with extra whipped cream and grated chocolate to serve.

53. Chocolate Hazelnut Mousse Recipe

Serving: 5 | Prep: | Cook: 15mins | Ready in:

Ingredients

- 1/4 cup sugar
- 1/4 cup unsweetened cocoa
- 2 1/2 tablespoons cornstarch
- 1/4 teaspoon salt
- 2 large eggs
- 2 cups 2% reduced-fat milk
- 1/4 cup Frangelico (hazelnut-flavored liqueur)
- 1/2 teaspoon vanilla extract
- 3 ounces bittersweet chocolate, chopped
- 2 cups frozen fat-free whipped topping, thawed
- 2 tablespoons chopped hazelnuts, toasted

Direction

- Combine the sugar, cocoa, cornstarch, salt, and eggs in a medium bowl, stirring well with a whisk.
- Heat milk over medium-high heat in a small, heavy saucepan to 180° or until tiny bubbles form around edge (do not boil).
- Gradually add hot milk to sugar mixture, stirring constantly with a whisk.
- Place the milk mixture in pan, and cook over medium heat until very thick and bubbly (about 5 minutes), stirring constantly.
- Spoon mixture into a medium bowl, and add liqueur, vanilla, and chocolate, stirring until chocolate melts.
- Place bowl in a large ice-filled bowl for 15 minutes or until mixture is cool, stirring occasionally.
- Remove bowl from ice.
- Gently fold in one-third of whipped topping. Fold in remaining topping.
- Cover and chill at least 3 hours. Sprinkle with hazelnuts.

54. Citrus Mousse Cheesecake Recipe

Serving: 0 | Prep: | Cook: 27mins | Ready in:

Ingredients

- Breton shortbread crust
- 80g un salted butter
- 105g flour
- 70g caster sugar
- 37g egg yolks
- 7g baking powder
- 50g ground almonds
- vanilla, to taste
- Mousse filling
- 250 cl l cream cheese
- 8 cl caster sugar
- 125g whipping cream 35.1%
- 1.5 gelatine sheets
- 3g orange and lemon zest flavouring
- vanilla, to taste
- almond essence, to taste

Direction

- Breton shortbread crust
- Blend the cold butter with the sugar and ground almonds
- Add the 2 egg yolks and the vanilla
- Add the sifted flour and baking powder
- Cover with cling film and chill
- Roll the dough in circles 5 mm thick
- Bake in individual 5 cm circle moulds at 170°C.
- Mousse filling
- Soften the Traditional Cream Cheese with a spatula
- Add the caster sugar and the citrus flavouring
- Incorporate the dissolved gelatine and the Elle &Vire Whipping Cream whipped until foamy
- Fill the shortbread bases and refrigerate
- Presentation
- Garnish with crystallised lemon slice

55. Classic Chocolate Mousse Recipe

Serving: 2 | Prep: | Cook: 120mins | Ready in:

Ingredients

- 2/3 cup chocolate (whatever kind you want, I just use chocolate chips)
- 1 tablespoon butter
- 3 large eggs, separated

Direction

- Put the chocolate in a saucepan over low heat until it is just melted.
- Remove the saucepan from heat and add in the butter. Leave for 1 minute, then stir in the egg YOLKS, one at a time.
- Put the mixture into a large bowl.
- In a separate bowl put the egg whites and using an electric whisk or mixer, whisk until stiff peaks form. The definition of stiff peaks is when you pull out your whisk or beater and the peaks do not sink back into the mixture after at least 20-30 seconds.
- STIR about ¼ of the egg whites into the butter and chocolate to loosen the mixture.
- Then, using a large metal spoon, FOLD in the rest of the egg whites (¼ at a time)
- Spoon into the cups you plan on eating them from. Then, chill for two hours. Eat in 12 hours.
- Bon appetit!

56. Cocoa Cappuccino Mousse Recipe

Serving: 0 | Prep: | Cook: 25mins | Ready in:

Ingredients

- 1 can (14 ounce) sweetened condensed milk
- 1/3 cup cocoa
- 3 tablespoons butter
- 2 teaspoons powdered instant coffee dissolved in 2 teaspoons hot water
- 2 cups, (1 pint) cold whipping cream

Direction

- 1. In a saucepan combine sweetened condensed milk, cocoa, butter and coffee in medium saucepan and cook over low heat stirring constantly until butter melts and mixture is smooth. Remove from the heat and cool.
- 2. Beat the whipping cream in a large bowl until stiff and then gradually fold into the chocolate a little at a time and then spoon into dessert bowls and refrigerate until set about 2 hours and garnish as desired.

57. Cocoa Mousse Recipe

Serving: 1 | Prep: | Cook: | Ready in:

Ingredients

- 1 banana (fully ripe)
- 1 tbsp of cocoa
- 1 tbsp of peanut butter
- a pinch of nigella

Direction

- Smash the banana adding cocoa and peanut butter until a creamy texture.
- Serve in a small cup, adding a pinch of nigella.

58. Coconut Mousse Recipe

Serving: 8 | Prep: | Cook: | Ready in:

Ingredients

- 1/4 cup butter, softened
- 1 tsp coconut or vanilla extract (I almost always use vanilla)
- 1 (8 oz) package cream cheese, softened
- 2/3 cup sugar
- 1 pint (2 cups) heavy whipping cream
- 1/2 cup sweetened flaked coconut
- toasted sweetened flaked coconut, for garnish

Direction

- Place butter, extract and cream cheese in large bowl. Beat at medium speed, scraping bowl often, until creamy. Add sugar; continue beating until well mixed.
- Increase speed to high. Beat, gradually adding whipping cream, until stiff peaks form. Gently stir in 1/2 cup flaked coconut by hand.
- To serve, divide mixture evenly among 8 individual serving dishes. Cover; refrigerate until serving time. Sprinkle with toasted coconut, if desired.

59. Coffee Chocolate Mousse Via Delta Point River Restaurant Recipe

Serving: 4 | Prep: | Cook: 5mins | Ready in:

Ingredients

- 4 egg yolks
- 3/4 cup sugar
- 1/4 cup Grand Marnier
- 6 ounces semi-sweet chocolate, in chunks
- 4 tablespoons brewed black coffee
- 6 ounces butter
- 4 egg whites
- 2 tablespoons confectioners' sugar

Direction

- In a double boiler, combine egg yolks, sugar and Grand Marnier.
- Heat until sugar melts thoroughly.
- In a separate pan, melt chocolate and coffee together.
- Add butter a little at a time.
- Mix thoroughly.
- Beat egg whites until stiff.
- Slowly add confectioners' sugar while continuing to beat.
- Combine egg yolk and chocolate mixtures and quickly into whites.
- Mix thoroughly and pour into individual serving dishes.
- Chill 2-4 hours immediately.
- Serve.

60. Cold Cherry Mousse With Vanilla Sauce Recipe

Serving: 6 | Prep: | Cook: 5mins | Ready in:

Ingredients

- vanilla Sauce:

- 4-1/2 teaspoons cherry brandy
- 3/4 cup low fat vanilla ice cream
- Mousse:
- 1 envelop whipped topping mix
- 1/2 cup low fat milk
- 1/2 teaspoon vanilla
- 2 envelopes unflavored gelatin
- 1/2 cup sugar
- 1/2 cup cold water
- 16 ounces frozen unsweetened cherries, thawed, undrained and divided
- 1 tablespoon fresh lemon juice
- 3/4 cup vanilla sauce

Direction

- Prepare whipped topping mix according to package directions using milk and vanilla.
- Set aside.
- Combine gelatine and sugar in a small saucepan, stir in water.
- Let stand 5 minutes to soften.
- Heat over low heat until gelatine is completely dissolved.
- Cool to room temperature.
- Set aside 1 cup of cherries without juice, for garnish.
- Place remaining cherries and juice into a blender.
- Add lemon juice and gelatine mixture.
- Process until blended.
- Fold cherry purée into whipped topping until no streaks of white show.
- Pour mixture into Bundt pan or ring mold.
- Refrigerate 4 hours or overnight until jelled.
- To serve, unmold mousse onto a large serving plate.
- Spoon remaining 1 cup of cherries into the center of mousse.
- Serve with vanilla sauce.
- Vanilla sauce:
- Stir brandy into low fat vanilla ice cream and blend well.
- Try adding some Grand Marnier into the sauce for a different flavor.

61. Comfort Mango Mousse Creamy Recipe

Serving: 4 | Prep: | Cook: 17mins | Ready in:

Ingredients

- 3 cups chopped ripe fresh mango or 2 cups mango puree.
- 1 can (2 cups) of sweetened condensed milk, chilled.
- 1 cup whipped cream.
- 2 tsp of grated lime peel.

Direction

- In a blender, process the mango until it makes a smooth puree, remove ¼ cup of the puree and add the condensed milk to the remaining and blend again.
- Take ½ cup of the whipped cream in a bowl and add the mango mixture over it and fold, until combined.
- Fill the dessert dishes with the mousse top it with 1 tbsp. of whipped cream and 1 tsp. of the mango puree.
- Sprinkle some lemon zest over it and Chill for at least an hour before serving.
- Have fun with your mango mousse. And try as many mango recipes as possible before the season is over.

62. Cool Whip Chocolate Mousse Recipe

Serving: 4 | Prep: | Cook: | Ready in:

Ingredients

- 1 (3.9 ounce) Package instant chocolate pudding mix (or get creative try a different flavor!)
- 1 1/2 Cups milk

- 1 (16 ounce) Whipped Toppping

Direction

- Prepare the pudding in large bowl, using the 1 1/2 cups instead of the 2 listed on the package
- Fold in the whipped topping until blended
- Refrigerate until chilled, then serve

63. Cranberry Mousse Recipe

Serving: 6 | Prep: | Cook: | Ready in:

Ingredients

- 1 cup boiling water
- 3 ounces cranberry raspberry flavored gelatin
- 16 ounces whole berry cranberry sauce
- 2 cups frozen whipped topping thawed
- 1/4 cup chopped toasted pecans

Direction

- Combine boiling water and gelatine stirring until dissolved then stir in cranberry sauce.
- Refrigerate until mixture mounds when dropped from a spoon about 30 minutes.
- Fold in whipped topping then spoon into serving dishes and sprinkle with pecans.
- Chill until set approximately 3 hours.

64. Cranberry Mousse With Chocolate Ganache Recipe

Serving: 6 | Prep: | Cook: | Ready in:

Ingredients

- Ganache Recipe
- 1/2 cup of heavy cream
- 1 cup of semi sweet or 8 oz of your best dark chocolate bar
- Mousse
- 1, 12 oz bag of fresh cranberries
- 2 cups of chilled heavy cream, whipped and mixed with 1 tsp. vanilla extract
- 1/2 cup of sugar
- 1/4 cup of water
- 1 tsp fresh lemon or orange zest
- (Taste your berry mixture. If you want it sweeter, add 1/4 cup of sugar. The chocolate adds sweetness to the complete recipe so taste both together before adding extra sugar please!)

Direction

- To make the ganache, simply add the chocolate to the cream in a microwave proof container and cook in microwave on high for 2 minutes.
- Stir until well blended and cool to room temperature.
- Do not refrigerate!
- Mousse
- Cook the cranberries with the sugar and water over medium heat until the berries pop. This takes about 10 minutes.
- Cook for five minutes after berries pop and remove from heat.
- Cool to room temperature.
- Crush the berries well using a fork and add the vanilla and zest.
- Gently fold in the berries into the whipped cream.
- To serve, add several tablespoons of ganache to the bottom of glass and top with the mousse. A dollop of whipped cream is a nice topped with some shaved chocolate. You can get between 4-8 servings of this depending on the glass you serve it in.
- *You can add a tablespoon of chocolate or orange liqueur to the mousse for a more adult flavour.

65. Cream From Heaven Natas Do Céu Recipe

Serving: 6 | Prep: | Cook: 40mins | Ready in:

Ingredients

- 1 package of Bolacha Maria cookies (about 16 cookies) - I did some research and you can sub Maria cookies for Nabisco tea cookies
- 1 pint of heavy cream
- 6 eggs, separated
- 2 tbs water
- 1/2 cup sugar plus 2 tbsp
- 1 teaspoon milk

Direction

- Roll out the cookies into fine crumbs and set aside.
- For the egg sweet topping
- In a small sauce pan, pour in 2 tablespoons of water and 1/4 cup of the sugar. Stir.
- Heat the sugar water until it forms a light threadlike syrup but do not boil or allow to become golden.
- In a small bowl, whisk the yolks with a teaspoon of the milk. Gradually, while still whisking, drizzle in the sugar syrup, incorporating it thoroughly into the yolks. Set aside.
- For the white mousse
- Beat the cream with 1/4 cup sugar until peaks form and set aside.
- In a separate bowl, beat the egg whites, until foamy. Continue to beat on high speed while gradually incorporating 2 tablespoons of sugar.
- Beat until soft peaks form.
- Fold the egg whites into the cream until the egg whites are thoroughly incorporated.
- To assemble
- Work in alternate layers starting on the bottom of glass bowl with the cookie crumbs. Pour a layer of cream followed by a layer of cookies until there's no more left of both then ending with topping it all with the sweetened egg yolks.

66. Creamy Cappuccino Mousse Recipe

Serving: 6 | Prep: | Cook: | Ready in:

Ingredients

- 1 -8oz package of softened cream cheese
- 1/2 cup cold milk
- 1 cup of strong brewed coffee
- 1 3.4 oz package of Jello instant vanilla pudding
- 1/4 tsp ground cinnamon
- 1 8oz carton of Cool Whip, thawed and divided

Direction

- In a large mixing bowl beat cream cheese until smooth.
- Slowly add milk, blend through then add in coffee.
- Add pudding mix and cinnamon and beat for about 2 minutes.
- Place in fridge for 5 minutes or until set.
- Fold in 2 cups of Cool Whip.
- Spoon into 6 pudding dishes and refrigerate until completely set.
- Garnish the remainder of the Cool Whip.
- Sprinkle on cinnamon atop if you wish.

67. Creamy White Mousse With Fresh Raspberries Recipe

Serving: 6 | Prep: | Cook: 5mins | Ready in:

Ingredients

- 3 bars (6oz) premiere white baking bars, broken into pieces
- 1 1/2 C. heavy whipping cream, divided
- 1/4 C. powdered sugar
- 1 tsp. vanilla
- fresh raspberries for garnish

Direction

- Microwave baking bars and 1/2 cup whipping cream in uncovered microwave safe bowl on medium-high heat until completely melted (approx. 90-120 seconds).
- Cool completely.
- Beat remaining 1 cup whipping cream, powdered sugar and vanilla in small bowl until stiff peaks form, but do NOT overbeat.
- Fold melted bar mixture into whipping cream mixture until blended.
- Spoon into champagne or wine glasses and chill until ready to serve.
- Garnish with fresh raspberries and watch their faces light up.
- YUM!!

68. Creme Au Chocolat Glace Aka Rich Chocolate Mousse Recipe

Serving: 4 | Prep: | Cook: 20mins | Ready in:

Ingredients

- 3 squares bitter chocolate (I use 6 Tablespoons Dutch cocoa + 2 T. butter)
- 2 Tablespoons butter
- 1/4 teaspoon cream of tartar
- 4 eggwhites
- 3 egg yolks
- 1/3 cup plus 1/4 cup granulated sugar
- 3 Tablespoons water
- 1 Tablespoon orange liqueur, kirsch, or Jamaican rum, or 2 teaspoons vanilla (I use the vanilla and the rum)

Direction

- Put the chocolate and butter in a double boiler to melt.
- Beat the egg whites until stiff, adding the cream tartar when foamy. When stiff, set aside
- Put 1/3 cup sugar and the 3 Tbsp. water in a small saucepan; bring to a boil. While beating the eggs, pour the boiling syrup in a small stream and incorporate the syrup into the whites. (If using processor to beat whites, pour syrup thru the feed tube)
- Process the yolks and the 1/4 cup sugar for 30 seconds. Remove the cover and add the melted butter and chocolate and also the flavourings. Process just long enough to blend, less than 10 seconds. Gently add the beaten whites into the chocolate mixture, folding into the chocolate until they just disappear. (Processor mode: when the whites are atop the chocolate butter mix, turn the machine on and off 2 or 3 times-just 'til whites disappear. Divide into 4 small bowls and refrigerate. It will solidify quickly.

69. Dark Chocolate Mousse Recipe

Serving: 6 | Prep: | Cook: 10mins | Ready in:

Ingredients

- half pound dark chocolate (suitable for cooking)
- 2 tea spoons butter
- 6 eggs
- 2 table spoons port wine

Direction

- Melt chocolate together with butter in bain-marie.
- Mix yolks with port wine.
- Whip egg whites into a firm foam.
- Now mix chocolate and yolks into a nice paste.
- Gently incorporate the egg whites (meringue) on the chocolate paste.

- Put it on a large bowl or 6 individual tiny bowls and cool it for at least 2 hours before serving.

70. Dark Chocolate Mousse With Baileys And Mascarpone Cream Recipe

Serving: 6 | Prep: | Cook: 60mins | Ready in:

Ingredients

- 3 free-range eggs
- 100 g caster sugar (or equivalent xylitol or stevia)
- 300 g dark chocolate, broken into small pieces
- 125 g unsalted butter
- 500 ml whipping cream
- cocoa powder, to finish (optional)
- For the Baileys cream:
- 200 g mascarpone cheese
- 75 ml Baileys
- 30 g caster sugar (or equivalent xylitol or stevia)

Direction

- Put the eggs and sugar in the bowl of an electric mixer and whisk until light and airy - the longer you whisk, the better, so give it at least eight to 10 minutes. (You could do it by hand, but that would be a big effort.)
- While the eggs are whisking, put the chocolate and butter in a heatproof bowl and place over a pan of barely simmering water. Stir with a wooden spoon until they melt completely.
- With the mixer running on medium speed, add the chocolate mix to the egg mix in a steady stream - it is important to combine the two gradually but continuously, with the chocolate going into the eggs and not the other way around.
- Whisk the cream until it firms up just a little - it needs to reach a loose ribbon stage (when you lift the whisk, the cream dribbling off should create clear lines in the surface before disappearing). Gently fold the semi-whipped cream into the egg and chocolate mix, and pour into a serving bowl. Chill for at least an hour to set.
- Make the Baileys cream in advance, or just before serving. Put all the ingredients in a bowl and whisk. The cheese will go loose and runny, but it should firm up again. Stop when it reaches a very soft peak consistency.
- Serve the mousse directly from the bowl with a huge dollop of Bailey's cream on top. Dust with cocoa powder, if you like.

71. Deadly Dark Chocolate Mousse Recipe

Serving: 0 | Prep: | Cook: 25mins | Ready in:

Ingredients

- http://baking.about.com
- Deadly Dark chocolate Mousse
- Ingredients
- •8 ounces bittersweet chocolate, chopped fine
- •2 tablespoons cocoa powder
- •1 teaspoon instant espresso powder (optional)
- •5 tablespoons water
- •1 tablespoon brandy (optional)
- •2 large eggs
- •1 tablespoon sugar, divided
- •1/4 teaspoon salt
- •1 cup plus 2 tablespoons whipping cream
- •Optional Toppings: additional whipped cream and cocoa powder

Direction

- Prep Time: 20 minutes
- Cook Time: 5 minutes
- Total Time: 25 minutes
- Yield: 6 - 8 servings
- Preparation

- In a double boiler over simmering water, melt chocolate, cocoa powder, espresso powder, water and brandy. Once melted, remove from heat.
- Separate eggs. Set egg whites aside. In a large bowl, whisk yolks with 2 teaspoons sugar and 1/4 teaspoon salt until combined and slightly thickened. Pour a little of the chocolate mixture into the egg yolk mixture. Whisk constantly. Add a little more chocolate and whisk.
- Add rest of chocolate mixture to the yolks. Set aside.
- In the clean dry bowl of a stand mixer, whisk egg whites until foamy. Add remaining teaspoon of sugar. Whisk whites until soft peaks form.
- Scoop 1/4 of egg whites into chocolate mixture and stir until combined. Add remaining egg whites and stir in a figure eight motion be sure to not over stir.
- In same stand mixer bowl, whip cream and remaining sugar. Fold whipped cream into chocolate mixture. Try not to over mix, but be sure to fold in all white portions.
- Either put all into a pretty serving bowl or into 6 to 8 individual bowls. Cover with plastic wrap and refrigerate from 2 to 24 hours prior to serving.
- Optional serving suggestion: Top with additional whipped cream and a sprinkling of cocoa power.

72. Dessert Recipe

Serving: 1 | Prep: | Cook: 1mins | Ready in:

Ingredients

- 100g dark chocolate with candied cherrys
- 100g cream
- 100g pistachio pudding allready made
- 50g sugar powder
- 50g sour cream
- maraschino cherrys, cream, milk chocolate sprinkles, coconut

Direction

- Melt the chocolate with cream. Pour in a glass, and set aside.
- Mix in a bowl, pudding, sour cream, sugar and add above chilled chocolate.
- Decorate with beaten cream, cherry, chocolate and coconut.

73. Disneys Jack Daniels Mousse Cake Recipe

Serving: 4 | Prep: | Cook: 10mins | Ready in:

Ingredients

- Bailey's Mousse (White Mousse)
- 2 egg yolks
- 4 ounces heavy cream
- 2 ounces white chocolate, melted
- 1/2 ounce Bailey's
- Leave gelatin in cold water, bloomed.
- ***
- Jack Daniels Mousse (Dark Mousse)*******************************
- 1 egg yolk
- 3 ounces heavy cream
- 1 ounce dark chocolate, melted
- 1/2 ounce Jack Daniels
- Leave gelatin in cold water, bloomed
- almond Sponge**************************
- 3 egg
- 3 ounces sugar
- 4 ounces almond finely chopped
- 3 egg whites
- 1 ounce sugar
- 1 ounce flour, all-purpose
- 1 ounce butter, melted

Direction

- - For Mousse

- . Whip the heavy cream in a bowl until thickened (soft peak).
- . Melt the chocolate in either a microwave or double boiler (be careful not to burn).
- . Bloom gelatine in ice water for 5 minutes.
- Dissolve the gelatine completely in the microwave.
- . In a bowl over a pan of simmering water, whip the egg yolks until pale in colour.
- Remove the egg yolks from the water bath and stir in the melted chocolate and a third of the heavy cream.
- . Return to the heat if necessary and stir until incorporated
- . Take the yolk mixture off the stove and whisk in the gelatine and alcohol.
- Fold in remaining cream.
- . Pour the white mousse half way into glass or bowl and chill.
- . Prepare dark chocolate mousse as below.
  ****
- For Dark Mousse
- . Mix sugar, egg, almond flour together.
- . Stir well.
- . Whip egg white and sugar to meringue.
- Fold into egg mixture.
- Bake at 350° F for about 9 minutes on baking sheet

74. Double Chocolate Velvet Mousse Recipe

Serving: 4 | Prep: | Cook: | Ready in:

Ingredients

- 200g milk chocolate melted
- 1cup sour cream
- 2 egg yolks
- 4 egg whites
- 1/4 cup caster sugar
- 200g white chocolate melted
- 1/2 cup double cream (whipped)
- 4 strawberries to decorate (sliced)

- 1 tablespoon shifted cocoa

Direction

- Combine milk chocolate with half the sour cream and one egg yolk in a large bowl, stir until smooth.
- Beat 2 egg whites until soft peak, gradually add half caster sugar and beat further 3 minutes; fold into chocolate mixture.
- Pour into 4 balloon glasses and chill till set
- To make white chocolate layer, combine white melted with the rest sour cream, and egg yolk and stir till smooth.
- Beat the remaining egg whites until soft peaks form gradually add in the sugar; beat for 3 minutes
- Fold into the white chocolate mixture and pour on top of the chilled milk chocolate mousse, chill till set
- Decorate with piped cream and strawberries dust with cocoa powder

75. Dutch Cocoa Mousse Slice With Ginger Bread Recipe Recipe

Serving: 6 | Prep: | Cook: 24hours | Ready in:

Ingredients

- Dutch honey bread
- 1 c brown sugar
- 2 c flour
- 1/2 c butter
- 1/2 t ginger
- 2 eggs
- 1/2 t cinnamon
- 1 t baking soda
- 1/2 t cloves
- 1/2 c honey
- 1/4 t salt
- 1/2 c buttermilk
- 1/2 c walnuts, chopped, tossed with
- 1 T flour
- Dutch cocoa mousse

- 200 g quark (smooth, fresh, low-fat, unripened cheese)
- 30 g Dutch cocoa
- 3 eggs, separated
- 60 g caster sugar
- a pinch of cream of tartar
- a little icing sugar for dusting
- 12 chocolate sticks flavoured with orange, for the garnish (optional)

Direction

- To Make Dutch Honey Bread
- Preheat oven to 350°F. Butter a loaf pan.
- In bowl, cream butter and sugar.
- Add in eggs.
- Mix the baking soda into the honey, then combine with the buttermilk.
- Sift the flour with the spices, and add the dry ingredients and wet ingredients alternately to the creamed butter mixture.
- Stir in the flour tossed nuts.
- Pour this into the prepared loaf pan.
- Rest on counter top for 20 minutes before baking.
- Place into preheated oven and bake until done, about 45 to 60 minutes. After bread is cooled, allow to "age" 24 hours before slicing and eating.
- To Make Dutch cocoa mousse
- Using a serrated knife, cut 18 slices of ginger bread about 5 mm thick.
- Place the quark and cocoa in a bowl and beat until combined. Add the 3 egg yolks and half the sugar and beat until smooth.
- Place the egg whites in a bowl with the cream of tartar and beat into stiff peaks. Add the remaining caster sugar and continue beating until smooth.
- Mix a little of the beaten egg whites into the cocoa mixture, then gently fold in remaining egg whites and mix until just combined.
- Place 6 slices of ginger bread on a large dish. Top each with 1 tbsp. of cocoa mousse, then with a second slice of ginger bread. Add another spoonful of mousse and finish with a slice of ginger bread. Spread a little extra mousse on the sides of the small cakes and dust the top with icing sugar. Refrigerate for at least 1 hour before serving.
- Garnish each slice with 2 orange sticks.

76. Easy Bittersweet Chocolate Mousse Cake Recipe

Serving: 6 | Prep: | Cook: | Ready in:

Ingredients

- 2 cups chilled heavy cream
- One 10-ounce jar bittersweet chocolate sauce (1 1/4 cups)
- One 9-ounce package chocolate wafers
- Shaved bittersweet chocolate, for garnish

Direction

- Beat heavy cream with the chocolate sauce at medium speed until firm peaks form.
- Put some saran wrap in a loaf pan with edges hanging out.
- Spread about 1/2 cup of the whipped chocolate cream on a long rectangular platter, to form a rectangle.
- Using a small offset spatula, spread 1 tablespoon of the remaining chocolate cream on 35 chocolate wafers and arrange them in 5 stacks.
- Top each stack with a chocolate wafer (you will have 6 or 7 wafers left over).
- Arrange the wafer stacks on their sides as close together as possible on the chocolate cream on the platter.
- Spread all but about 1/2 cup of the remaining chocolate cream all over the cake, fixing any wafers that tilt or slide.
- Press a long sheet of plastic wrap over the cake, flattening the top and sides gently.
- Refrigerate for at least 8 hours or for up to 2 days.
- Refrigerate the remaining chocolate cream.

- Remove the saran wrap and frost the cake with the remaining chocolate cream.
- Garnish with the chocolate shavings.

77. Easy Chocolate Mousse Recipe

Serving: 8 | Prep: | Cook: 10mins | Ready in:

Ingredients

- 150 gms marshmallows
- 50 gms butter
- 250 gms semi-sweet chocolate chips
- 4 table spoons hot water
- 280 ml whipping cream, whipped
- Flaked almonds

Direction

- On the stove, put together the marshmallows and the butter and the chocolate chips and the hot water until the marshmallows and the chocolate chips have disappeared.
- Remove from the stove and carefully fold in the whipped whipping cream.
- Cool for 1 hour.
- Garnish with flaked almonds and serve immediately.
- NOTE: do not cool overnight as the mousse will harden.

78. Easy Double Chocolate Mousse Recipe

Serving: 8 | Prep: | Cook: 20mins | Ready in:

Ingredients

- 1 16 ounce cool whip whipped topping, fat free
- 1 15 ounce chocolate sweetened condensed milk
- 1 8 ounce package fat free or low fat cream cheese
- 1/4 to 1/2 cup Hershey's Cocoa Special Dark, to taste (the powder not the solid)
- 1 11 ounce package peanut butter chips, you can use dark chocolate chips or any flavor really.

Direction

- Mix together cream cheese and chocolate sweetened condensed milk.
- Add dark chocolate baking powder
- Fold in the cool whip.
- Gently fold in your choice of chips.
- Serve as is or put mixture into a chocolate graham cracker crust.
- Or just serve in a bowl with graham crackers on the side as the spoon.
- Chill and enjoy.

79. Easy Pumpkin Mousse Recipe

Serving: 4 | Prep: | Cook: | Ready in:

Ingredients

- 1-1/2 cups cold fat-free milk
- 1 package (1 ounce) sugar-free instant butterscotch pudding mix
- 1/2 cup canned pumpkin
- 1/2 teaspoon ground cinnamon
- 1/4 teaspoon ground ginger
- 1/4 teaspoon ground allspice
- 1 cup fat-free whipped topping, divided

Direction

- In a large bowl, whisk milk and pudding mix for 2 minutes.
- Let stand for 2 minutes or until soft-set.
- Combine the pumpkin, cinnamon, ginger and allspice; fold into pudding.
- Fold in 1/2 cup whipped topping.
- Transfer to individual serving dishes.

- Refrigerate until serving.
- Garnish with remaining whipped topping.

80. Easy Raspberry Iced Mousse Recipe

Serving: 4 | Prep: | Cook: 5mins | Ready in:

Ingredients

- 2x250g tubs of quark (Take 9 parts of ricotta cheese and 1 part of sour cream and blend together)
- 50g icing sugar
- A squeeze or 2 of fresh lemon juice
- 250g frozen raspberries

Direction

- Tip the quark or ricotta mixture into a bowl with the sugar and lemon juice, beat with a wooden spoon until smooth and creamy Gently stir in the berries until they begin to break up and the cheese is streaked pink. Taste and add more lemon juice if liked.
- Note: I have never used the ricotta +sour cream before but have been told by friends it works just as well.

81. Easy Strawberry Mousse Recipe

Serving: 8 | Prep: | Cook: | Ready in:

Ingredients

- 4 cups quartered fresh strawberries or frozen unsweetened strawberries
- 1/2 cup sugar
- 1 package (1 ounce) sugar-free instant vanilla pudding mix
- 1 carton (8 ounces) frozen reduced-fat whipped topping, thawed

Direction

- In a food processor or blender, combine strawberries and sugar; cover and process until smooth.
- Strain and discard seeds.
- Return strawberry mixture to the food processor. Add pudding mix; cover and process until smooth.
- Transfer to a large bowl; fold in whipped topping.
- Spoon into dessert dishes.
- Refrigerate until serving.
- Yield: 8 servings.

82. Easy White Chocolate Mousse Recipe

Serving: 0 | Prep: | Cook: 15mins | Ready in:

Ingredients

- 7 ounces white chocolate
- 2 egg yolks
- 2 tablespoons sugar
- 1/4 cup heavy cream, plus 1 cup
- powdered sugar and fruit for garnish

Direction

- Put the white chocolate in a medium to large sized bowl.
- Add the egg yolks and sugar to a small bowl and whisk until pale in colour.
- In a saucepan, over low heat, bring 1/4 cup of the cream to a simmer, and SLOWLY add the cream into the yolk and sugar mixture. Pour the creamy mixture back into pan and stir with a wooden spoon until it coats the back of it.
- Pour hot mix into the bowl with the chopped chocolate. Stir until completely smooth.
- In another bowl, whip remaining 1 cup of the cream until it's the consistency of whipped cream. Fold half the whipped cream into the

white chocolate mix to lighten and then fold in the remaining whipped cream.
- Spoon the white chocolate mousse into 4 serving cups and refrigerate until set, approximately 1 hour.
- Garnish each serving with powdered and any fruit of your liking.

83. Eggnog Mousse Recipe

Serving: 5 | Prep: | Cook: 120mins | Ready in:

Ingredients

- 2 cups cold eggnog
- 1-1/2 cups cold milk
- 2 pkg. (4-serving size each) vanilla flavor instant pudding & pie filling
- 1/4 tsp. ground nutmeg
- 2-1/2 cups thawed French vanilla flavored whipped topping, divided

Direction

- Pour eggnog and milk into large bowl.
- Add dry pudding mixes and nutmeg. Beat with wire whisk 2 min. or until well blended.
- Gently stir in 1-1/2 cups of the whipped topping.
- Spoon evenly into 5 dessert dishes or 1-1/2-qt. serving bowl; cover.
- Refrigerate at least 2 hours.
- Top evenly with the remaining 1 cup whipped topping just before serving.
- Sprinkle with additional nutmeg, if desired.

84. Fake Out Mousse Recipe

Serving: 6 | Prep: | Cook: | Ready in:

Ingredients

- 1 package of instant pudding mix (reccomend vanilla or chocolate or variation of one of them)
- 1-1/2 Cups cold milk
- 1 tub of Cool Whip

Direction

- Prepare pudding according to directions using only 1-1/2 cups of milk instead of two.
- Gently fold in cool whip, chill in fridge for 30 minutes.
- Serve over angel food or pound cake with fresh berries if desired. Enjoy!
- **Note: When using vanilla I use vanilla cool whip.
- **Note: When using chocolate I use chocolate milk and chocolate cool whip. Enjoy!

85. French Vanilla Custard Mousse Recipe

Serving: 12 | Prep: | Cook: 20mins | Ready in:

Ingredients

- 2 cups 18% cream
- 1 vanilla bean, scraped
- 6 eggs, separated
- 2/3 cup superfine sugar, separated
- 1/4 cup cornstarch
- 1/4 tsp salt
- 1/2 tsp cream of tartar

Direction

- Scald the cream, vanilla seeds and vanilla pod in a heavy saucepan. Remove from heat, remove vanilla pod and set aside to cool slightly.
- Meanwhile, beat egg yolks and 1/3 cup sugar in a bowl until the mixture is creamy and pale yellow, and the mixture leaves a "ribbon trail" when the whisk/beaters are lifted.
- Beat in the cornstarch.

- Slowly add a ladle of the hot cream mixture to the beaten yolks, whisking constantly, to bring them to temperature, then slowly pour the yolk mixture into the pot with the remaining hot cream, still beating constantly.
- Return pot to medium heat, whisking constantly (it will thicken as it reaches a boil).
- Reduce the heat to low and continue to cook for 2 minutes more, stirring constantly all the while. Remove from heat and strain into a cold bowl.
- In a clean bowl, whip egg whites with cream of tartar and remaining sugar until stiff peaks form.
- Fold half the whites into the custard mixture to lighten it, then scrape the remaining whites in and gently but quickly fold them in until well mixed but not deflated.
- Chill before serving.

86. Fresh Rasberry Mousse Recipe

Serving: 12 | Prep: | Cook: | Ready in:

Ingredients

- 3 1/2 pints raspberries
- 10 egg whites, room temperature
- 1/4 lb superfine sugar or to taste
- 1/4 tsp cream of tarter
- 1/2 oz Chambord (raspberry liquer)
- 3 pints heavy cream whipped
- fresh raspberries for garnish

Direction

- Puree berries in processor and strain to remove seeds.
- Beat egg white with cream of tartar till stiff.
- Gradually add sugar to whites while beating.
- Fold raspberries into whipped cream and then fold in egg whites.
- Pour or pipe into dessert glasses.
- Garnish with some fresh raspberries.
- Serve at once or chill

- Yield, 12, 8 1/2 oz. servings

87. Frozen Chocolate Mousse Squares Recipe

Serving: 16 | Prep: | Cook: 10mins | Ready in:

Ingredients

- 12 OREO chocolate Sandwich cookies, crushed
- 1/4 cup (1/2 stick) butter or margarine, melted
- 2 containers (8 oz. each) cream cheese spread
- 1 can (14 oz.) sweetened condensed milk
- 4 squares Semi-Sweet baking chocolate, melted
- 1 cup thawed Cool Whip whipped topping

Direction

- MIX crushed cookies and the butter in foil-lined 9-inch square pan. Press firmly onto bottom of pan to form crust.
- BEAT cream cheese in large bowl with electric mixer on low speed until creamy. Gradually add milk, mixing well after each addition. Blend in chocolate. Gently stir in whipped topping. Spoon over crust; cover.
- FREEZE at least 6 hours or overnight. Remove from freezer 15 min. before serving to soften slightly. Cut into 16 squares to serve. Store leftover dessert in freezer.

88. Frozen Mint Chocolate Mousse Recipe

Serving: 6 | Prep: | Cook: | Ready in:

Ingredients

- 1 can (300 mL) Regular or Low Fat Eagle Brand® sweetened condensed milk

- 2/3 cup (150 mL) chocolate syrup
- 1 tsp (5 mL) peppermint extract
- 1 cup (250 mL) whipping cream, whipped

Direction

- In large bowl, combine Eagle Brand, syrup and peppermint extract. Fold in whipped cream.
- Spoon equal portions into 6 or 8 individual serving dishes.
- Freeze 3 to 4 hours or until firm.
- Garnish as desired.
- Serve immediately.
- *Optional garnishes:
- Chocolate shavings, whipped cream, a mint leaf, a mint truffle, a chopped York Mint patty, a chocolate or vanilla wafer, an Oreo cookie, a few mini marshmallows.
- (I added a cup of mini marshmallows to this recipe and it came out great! You get more mousse and a lighter texture.)

89. Fudgy Peanut Butter Mousse Cups Recipe

Serving: 36 | Prep: | Cook: 70mins | Ready in:

Ingredients

- 1 (17.5 oz.) pkg sugar cookie mix
- 1c pecans, toasted and chopped fine
- 2Tbs. flour
- 8Tbs (1 stick) unsalted butter, melted
- 1 1/4c heavy cream
- 1c chunky peanut butter
- 1 (8oz) pkg. cream cheese, softened
- 1c confectioners' sugar
- 1tsp. vanilla extract
- 1c semi-sweet chocolate chips

Direction

- Adjust oven rack to middle position and heat oven to 350. Grease a 12 cup mini-muffin tin. Combine cookie mix, pecans, and flour in a bowl. Slowly stir in butter until mixture resembles wet sand. Press 1
- Tbs. cookie mixture into bottom and sides of each muffin cup. Bake until golden, about 10 mins. Cool 20 mins. In tin, then turn out cookies. Repeat with remaining dough.
- With electric mixer on med-high speed, beat 1 cup cream to stiff peaks, about 2 mins. In another bowl, beat peanut butter, cream cheese, sugar, and vanilla on med. speed till smooth, about 1 min. Fold in whipped cream.
- Microwave chocolate and remaining cream in small bowl, stirring occasionally till smooth, about 1 min. Pour 1/2tsp chocolate mixture in each cookie cup, then fill cups with 1 Tbs. peanut butter mixture. Drizzle remaining chocolate evenly over cookies and refrigerate till firm, about 1 hour.

90. Ganache / Mousse! Recipe

Serving: 4 | Prep: | Cook: 15mins | Ready in:

Ingredients

- 500 g dark chocolate, or 625g milk/white chocolate finely chopped (or chips)
- 500 mL cream
- 1T corn syrup
- vanilla, coffee, cointreau, kirsch, Frangelico, any flavoring desired.

Direction

- Boil 250mL cream with corn syrup.
- Pour over chocolate and let sit for around 3-5 minutes
- Gently stir with whisk until incorporated. Voila, Smooth Glossy Ganache!
- Let sit until room temp
- MEANWHILE.... whip up cream (sometimes I use a packet of whip it too, this works well when you are using the mousse as a filling for a cake!)

- When ganache is cool, fold into whipped cream with whisk and pour into ramekin/bowl/pastry/whatever!
- Sets in about 25-30 minutes

91. German Chocolate Mousse Recipe

Serving: 8 | Prep: | Cook: 3hours | Ready in:

Ingredients

- 1 1/3 cups 1% low-fat milk
- 2 teaspoons unflavored gelatin
- 1 teaspoon vanilla extract
- 8 ounces dark chocolate chips
- 4 cups frozen light whipped topping, thawed
- 1/4 cup flaked sweetened coconut. toasted (optional)
- 1/4 cup chopped pecans, toasted (optional)

Direction

- 1. Combine first 3 ingredients in a heavy saucepan; let stand 2 minutes. Cook over medium-high heat to180 degrees or until tiny bubbles for around the edge (do not boil). Remove from heat, and add chocolate; cover and let stand 5 minutes. Stir until chocolate melts.
- 2. Pour chocolate mixture into a medium bowl; cover and chill 30 minutes or until set. Gently fold in whipped topping. Spoon about 2/3 cup mousse into each of 8 dessert bowls. Cover and chill 2 hours or until set. Top each serving with 1 1/2 teaspoons coconut and 1 1/2 teaspoons pecans

92. Ginger And Caramel Mousse Recipe

Serving: 5 | Prep: | Cook: 20mins | Ready in:

Ingredients

- 6 egg yolks
- pinch of salt
- 1 packet unflavored gelatin
- 3/4 cup water, divided
- 1 cup sugar
- 1 tsp ginger (1/2 tsp more if you really like ginger)
- 2 cups heavy cream

Direction

- In the bowl of a stand mixer, whisk the egg yolks and the salt. In a small bowl, sprinkle the gelatine over 1/4 cup water, and let it sit while you make the caramel.
- Combine the sugar, ginger and 1/4cup water in a heavy saucepan. Cover and bring to a rapid boil over medium high heat (prevents crystallization of the sugar on the side of the pan).
- Once boiling, uncover and cook the sugar until deep golden brown. Turn off the heat and carefully pour 1/4 cup water into the hot caramel.
- The syrup will bubble and spurt, so stand back.
- Make sure the water incorporates fully to the syrup.
- Return to the heat if you get caramel bits and stir until it is one smooth liquid.
- Pour the caramel slowly and into a steady stream into the egg yolks with the machine running on medium high.
- Melt the gelatine in the microwave for 10 seconds or into the (now empty) saucepan until dissolved.
- Add it to the yolk mixture and continue to whisk on medium high until it triples in volume and cools to room temperature.
- In a separate bowl, whip the heavy cream to soft peaks.
- Add it to the mousse base and fold the two gently together.

- Divide the mousse into cups, ramequins, dishes, etc...And let it set, covered in the refrigerator for at least 2 hours.

93. Grasshopper Mousse Recipe

Serving: 4 | Prep: | Cook: 20mins | Ready in:

Ingredients

- 1-1/2 cups cold milk, divided
- 2 squares BAKER'S Semi-Sweet baking chocolate
- 1 pkg. (4-serving size) JELL-O chocolate Flavor Instant Pudding & pie filling
- 2 cups thawed Cool Whip whipped topping, divided
- 2 3 Muskateers mint chocolate bars (Frozen!)

Direction

- COMBINE 1 cup of the milk and chocolate in large microwavable bowl. Microwave on HIGH 2 min. Stir until chocolate is completely melted. Stir in remaining 1/2 cup milk.
- ADD dry pudding mix; beat with wire whisk 2 min. or until well blended. Refrigerate 20 minutes. Gently stir in 1-1/2 cups of the whipped topping. Spoon into 6 dessert dishes.
- REFRIGERATE until ready to serve. Top with remaining whipped topping.
- CHOP 3 Musketeers bars in a blender until about the size of chocolate chips. Sprinkle candy bar pieces on top of mousse. Add some dark chocolate shavings for added oomph!

94. Graveyard Pumpkin Mousse Recipe

Serving: 8 | Prep: | Cook: | Ready in:

Ingredients

- 12 chocolate sandwich cookies
- 1 cup heavy cream
- 1 package (8 ounces) reduced-fat cream cheese, softened
- 3/4 cup sugar
- 1 can (15 ounces) solid-pack pumpkin
- 1 teaspoon pumpkin pie spice
- 3 medium bananas, cut into 1/4" thick slices
- Long gummy worms and clean plastic skeletons or spiders, for garnish

Direction

- Process the cookies in a food processor bowl fitted with a steel blade to make fine crumbs; set aside. Beat the cream in a mixing bowl to form firm peaks; set aside. Beat the cream cheese and sugar in a separate bowl until creamy. Add the pumpkin and pumpkin pie spice; mix well. Fold in the whipped cream and bananas until blended to finish the mousse.
- Spoon 3/4 cup pumpkin mousse into each of 8 stemmed dessert glasses or large custard cups; spread top evenly. Sprinkle 2 tablespoons cookie crumbs over the top. Cover and refrigerate until serving time. To garnish, arrange gummy worms and skeletons on "dirt" layer, arranging gummy worms to resemble worms crawling out of the glass.
- Tip: If a food processor is not available, place the cookies in a resealable plastic bag. Close securely; crush with a rolling pin or meat mallet to make fine crumbs.
- Nutritional Information Per Serving: 381 calories; 21g fat; 61mg cholesterol; 372mg sodium; 45g carbohydrate; 3g fibre; 6g protein.

95. Guinness Black And White Mousse Recipe

Serving: 8 | Prep: | Cook: 35mins | Ready in:

Ingredients

- Black chocolate Mousse
- 8 ounces semisweet or bittersweet chocolate, chopped or grated
- 1/2 c (1 stick) unsalted Kerrygold butter
- 1/4 C sugar
- 3/4 C Guinness
- 3 Lrg eggs, separated
- 1 C heavy cream
- white chocolate Mousse
- 6 ounces white chocolate, chopped or grated
- 1 c heavy cream

Direction

- Black Chocolate Mousse
- In a small bowl set over simmering water, or in a double boiler, combine the chocolate, butter and sugar. Stir until the chocolate has melted and the mixture is smooth.
- Stir in Guinness and whisk in the egg yolks
- Remove from heat
- In a small bowl, whip the cream with an electric mixer until soft peaks form
- Fold the cream into the chocolate mixture
- With clean medium bowl and beaters, beat the egg whites until stiff peaks form
- Fold whites into the chocolate mixture
- Fill 8 parfait or wine glasses 3/4 full with the chocolate mixture and refrigerate while preparing the white chocolate mousse.
- White Chocolate Mousse
- In a small saucepan over medium heat, combine the white chocolate and 1/2 C of the cream
- Stir until the chocolate has melted and the mixture is smooth
- Remove from heat and let cool, stirring once or twice, for 30 minutes, or until thickened.
- In a small bowl beat the remaining 1/2 c of cream until stiff peaks form
- Fold the whipped cream into the white chocolate mixture
- Spoon the mixture over the top of the chocolate mousses and refrigerate at least 2 hours, but no more than 24 hours.

96. HAZELNUT MOUSSE Recipe

Serving: 8 | Prep: | Cook: | Ready in:

Ingredients

- 1 13 ounce jar of nutella hazelnut spread
- 1 16 ounce container of Cool Whip dessert topping
- (or use real whipped cream instead)
- 8 ounces Oreo cookies, crushed
- whipped cream to garnish

Direction

- Mix the Nutella with the Cool Whip until well blended.
- In a parfait glass, put a spoon full of crushed Oreo cookies.
- Add a layer of the hazelnut/Cool Whip mixture.
- Top with another spoonful of crushed Oreo cookies.
- Continue layering until full.
- Top with whipped cream.
- Note: Small parfait glasses work best as this is a rich dessert!

97. Harvest Mousse With Spiced Almond Tuiles Recipe

Serving: 10 | Prep: | Cook: 80mins | Ready in:

Ingredients

- 4 hours chill time
- MOUSSE
- 2 medium butternut squash (3 pounds), halved lengthwise and seeded
- 1/2 cup superfine sugar
- 2 tablespoons pure maple syrup
- 1/4 teaspoon each of ground cloves, ginger, cardamom, nutmeg and allspice

- 1 envelope unflavored powdered gelatin
- 2 tablespoons cold water
- 3 large egg whites
- 1 cup heavy cream
- candiED squash
- 1/2 cup sugar
- 1/2 cup water
- 1/2 vanilla bean, split, seeds scraped
- 1/2 teaspoon freshly ground pepper
- 1 cup diced peeled butternut squash (1/2-inch cubes)
- Lightly sweetened whipped cream and Spiced almond Tuiles, for serving

Direction

- Directions
- MAKE THE MOUSSE:
- Preheat the oven to 350°. Place the squash, cut side down, on a lightly oiled baking sheet. Bake for about 1 hour, until very tender. Let cool slightly, then scoop out the flesh.
- In a food processor, combine 3 cups of the squash with 5 tablespoons of the superfine sugar and the maple syrup; puree until smooth. In a small bowl, stir together the ground spices; add them to the squash puree and pulse to blend.
- In a small microwave-safe bowl, sprinkle the gelatine over the cold water and let stand until softened, 2 to 3 minutes. Melt the gelatine in a microwave oven at high power, about 10 seconds. Add the gelatine to the squash puree and pulse to combine. Scrape the puree into a large bowl.
- In a medium bowl, using a handheld electric mixer, beat the egg whites at medium speed until soft peaks form. With the mixer on, add the remaining 3 tablespoons of superfine sugar and beat until the whites are stiff and glossy. Fold the egg whites into the squash. Pour the heavy cream into the bowl the whites were in and beat at medium speed until firm. Fold the whipped cream into the mousse. Spoon the mousse into 10 parfait glasses and refrigerate until firm, at least 4 hours

98. Hazelnut And Chocolate Mousse Recipe

Serving: 6 | Prep: | Cook: 5mins | Ready in:

Ingredients

- 1/3 cup sugar OR Splenda Granulated Sweetener
- 1/3 cup unsweetened cocoa
- 2 1/2 tablespoons cornstarch
- 1/4 teaspoon salt
- 2 large eggs
- 2 cups 2% reduced-fat milk
- 1/3 cup Frangelico (hazelnut-flavored liqueur)
- 1/2 teaspoon vanilla extract
- 3 ounces bittersweet chocolate, chopped
- 2 cups frozen fat-free whipped topping, thawed
- 2 tablespoons chopped hazelnuts, toasted OR chocolate shavings

Direction

- Combine the sugar, cocoa, cornstarch, salt, and eggs in a medium bowl, stirring well with a whisk.
- Heat milk over medium-high heat in a small, heavy saucepan to 180° or until tiny bubbles form around edge (do not boil). Gradually add hot milk to sugar mixture, stirring constantly with a whisk. Place the milk mixture in pan, and cook over medium heat until very thick and bubbly (about 5 minutes), stirring constantly. Spoon mixture into a medium bowl, and add liqueur, vanilla, and chocolate, stirring until chocolate melts. Place bowl in a large ice-filled bowl for 15 minutes or until mixture is cool, stirring occasionally.
- Remove bowl from ice. Gently fold in one-third of whipped topping. Fold in remaining topping. Cover and chill at least 3 hours. Sprinkle with hazelnuts.
- Serving size: about 2/3 cup mousse and 1 teaspoon hazelnuts

99. Hazelnut Chocolate Mousse Recipe Recipe

Serving: 8 | Prep: | Cook: 30mins | Ready in:

Ingredients

- 2 cups heavy cream
- 4 egg yolks
- 3 tablespoons granulated sugar
- 2 tablespoons Frangelico (hazelnut liquor)
- 7 ounces bittersweet chocolate, melted and kept lukewarm
- 1/3 cup chopped, toasted hazelnuts

Direction

- Heat 2/3 cup of cream in small saucepan until it just begins to steam. In a separate bowl, whisk together the egg yolks and sugar, and then add ½ cup hot cream, whisking constantly, until the mixture is thoroughly combined. Add the warm egg-cream blend back into the hot cream in the saucepan and cook over low heat, stirring constantly, until the mixture reaches 165 degrees on a candy thermometer. Remove from the heat and stir in the hazelnut liquor and melted chocolate. Chill the chocolate custard thoroughly.
- Beat remaining 1 1/3 cups of cream in a separate bowl until stiff peaks form. Thoroughly stir ½ cup of the whipped cream into the chilled chocolate custard, and then gently fold in the remaining cream.
- The chocolate mousse is ready when the chocolate custard is thoroughly incorporated into the whipped cream, and no marbling shows. Serve chilled garnished with toasted hazelnuts.

100. Hoochs Rich Chocolate Mousse Recipe

Serving: 4 | Prep: | Cook: 7mins | Ready in:

Ingredients

- 250 grams dark chocolate
- ¼ cup Baileys Irish Cream liquer
- ¼ cup cream
- 3 eggs, separated
- 1 cup cream, whipped

Direction

- 1. Place chocolate, Baileys and first measure cream in a heatproof bowl over a saucepan of hot water.
- 2. Melt the chocolate over a low heat, leave to cool for 5 to 10 minutes. Add egg yolks to the chocolate mixture, beating well.
- 3. In a clean bowl, whisk the egg whites until soft peaks form. Fold the cream into the chocolate mixture, carefully fold in the egg whites.
- 4. Pour into glasses and chill to set.
- 5. Garnish with chocolate curls.
- Note: For a rich tasting chocolate, look for one that has over 60% cocoa solids, Use white chocolate in place of dark as a variation.

101. Hybiscus Flower Gelatine With Lychee Mousse Recipe

Serving: 6 | Prep: | Cook: 10mins | Ready in:

Ingredients

- *gelatine
- 1 oz dried hybiscus petals
- 2 leaves or 1/2 small packet unflavored gelatine powder
- 8 Tbsp granulated sugar
- *Mousse

- 2 leaves or 1/2 small packet unflavored gelatine powder
- 14 oz lychees, peeled and stones removed
- 5 oz whipping cream
- 1 medium egg white
- *For final assembly and decoration
- 6 extra lychees, peeled and stones removed
- 2 1/2 oz piece of good quality sponge cake

Direction

- * Gelatine:
- Boil 9 oz. water, then turn off heat.
- Add hibiscus petals and then cover pot for 10 minutes.
- Strain petals and add sugar to liquid.
- Heat gently, stirring until sugar is dissolved.
- Add gelatine and stir until dissolved.
- Divide into 6 ramekins or 6 small dessert cups.
- Chill until set.
- * Mousse:
- Puree the 14 ounces of lychees.
- Gently heat a few tablespoons of the lychees in a small saucepan.
- Add the gelatine powder to the heated lychees and mix thoroughly.
- Mix the heated lychee/gelatine with the remainder of the pureed lychees.
- Set aside for 1 hour to let it partially set.
- Whisk the cream until it forms soft peaks.
- Whisk the egg white until peaks form.
- Boil 5 Tbsp. of sugar with 1 Tbsp. of water until dissolved.
- Whisk into egg white.
- Fold whipped cream into lychee mixture, then fold into the meringue.
- To assemble:
- Roughly chop the remaining 6 lychees and cut the cake into small cubes.
- Put 3-4 cubes on top of the hibiscus gelatine and add a spoonful of chopped lychee.
- Divide the mousse among the 6 individual cups.
- Chill until set.

102. Island Creams Recipe

Serving: 8 | Prep: | Cook: | Ready in:

Ingredients

- 4 tablespoons thick honey
- 4 size 2 egg yolks
- ½ pint double cream
- 4 tablespoons whisky
- grated chocolate

Direction

- Heat the honey in a pan until it's hot and runny. Beat the egg yolks and then slowly add the honey until the mixture becomes pale and thick and like mousse. Whip the double cream and slowly whip in the whisky. Fold together the egg yolk mixture and the cream. Divide into 8 ramekins dishes, sprinkle with the grated chocolate, put on a tray, cover and freeze.

103. Jello Chocolate Mousse Recipe

Serving: 5 | Prep: | Cook: 15mins | Ready in:

Ingredients

- 1 small package jello chocolate pudding mix
- 1 tablespoon cocoa powder
- 12 oz soft tofu
- 1 teaspoon vanilla
- 8 oz whipping cream

Direction

- Combine the jello pudding and tofu. Add the cocoa and mix until stiff. Stir in the vanilla. Add the whipping cream and mix until blended.
- Warning: Do not mix it for too long, or else you will end up with a butter consistency, which is too thin.

- Divide the mixture between individual serving dishes and chill for a few hours or overnight. You can garnish each mousse with some cream, a raspberry, and a sprig of mint if you want to impress.

104. Kahlua Mousse Recipe

Serving: 12 | Prep: | Cook: 20mins | Ready in:

Ingredients

- 1c sugar
- 1c water
- 1 pint whipping cream
- 4 eggs
- 12 oz.(2c) semi-sweet chocolate chips
- das of salt
- 1/3c Kahlua
- 1/8c cognac

Direction

- In medium sauce pan, combine sugar and water. Heat slowly till sugar is completely melted and very hot, about 5 mins.
- In bowl of electric mixer, whip cream till stiff peaks form. Set aside.
- In blender combine eggs, chocolate chips, and salt. On lowest speed, in a slow, steady stream, add sugar mixture. Blend till smooth. Add Kahlua and cognac. Mix well.
- In large bowl, place 3 cups whipped cream. Fold in chocolate mixture till mixed well
- Pour mixture into individual serving dishes, a mould or a large serving bowl. Chill till set, at least 3 hours.
- To serve, top with remaining whipped cream.

105. Kamora Chocolate Mousse Recipe

Serving: 4 | Prep: | Cook: 15mins | Ready in:

Ingredients

- 1/4 c Kamora coffee liqueur
- 1/4 c splenda
- 4 oz semi sweet chocolate chips
- 3 tbsp cream
- 2 egg whites, beaten stiff
- 1 c whipping cream, beaten

Direction

- In saucepan over very low heat, mix Kamora and sugar, stir until sugar is dissolved
- Remove from heat
- Melt chocolate and cream in top of double boiler and mix until smooth, remove from heat and cool for 20 mins
- Stir chocolate into Kamora mixture
- Carefully fold in egg whites, then whipped cream
- Chill 3 hours before serving.

106. Key Lime Mousse Cups Recipe

Serving: 30 | Prep: | Cook: 20mins | Ready in:

Ingredients

- 4 oz cream cheese, softened
- 2/3 c sweetened condensed milk
- 1/4 c key lime juice
- 1/2 c heavy cream, whipped
- 2 pkgs (1.9 oz. ea) frozen miniature phyllo tart shells
- fresh raspberries and lime wedges

Direction

- In large bowl, beat cream cheese, milk and juice until smooth; fold in whipped cream. Pipe into tart shells.
- Garnish with raspberries and lime wedges, if desired.
- Serve immediately.

107. Key Lime Mousse Recipe

Serving: 4 | Prep: | Cook: 5mins | Ready in:

Ingredients

- 1/2 tablespoon grated key lime zest
- 1/2 cup fresh key lime juice
- 1/2 cup granulated sugar
- pinch of salt
- 3 large eggs
- 3/4 stick butter, cut into bits
- 2/3 cups chilled heavy cream

Direction

- Whisk together zest, juice, sugar, salt and eggs in small heavy saucepan.
- Add butter and cook over medium-low heat, whisking frequently, until it thickens (about 5 minutes).
- Force through fine-mesh sieve into a bowl, then quick chill in an ice bath.
- Stir occasionally for about 5 minutes.
- Beat cream until it holds stiff peaks, then fold into custard gently but thoroughly.
- Spoon into glasses and chill at least 2 hours.

108. Key Lime Mousse With Jetts Gingersnap Cookies Recipe

Serving: 8 | Prep: | Cook: 20mins | Ready in:

Ingredients

- 1 teaspoon unflavored gelatin
- 1/4 cup boiling water
- 1 can(12 fl. oz) evaporated milk
- 4 oz. cream cheese, softened
- 1 jar (7oz.) marshmallow cream
- 1/3 cup powdered sugar
- 2 tablespoons key lime juice
- 2 teaspoons key lime zest (Use microplane for extra fine zest)
- Additonal lime zest(optional)
- ***8 gingersnaps cookies*****
- Refer to "Only a Matter of Time Before Gingersnaps" cookie recipe on my food page.
- (you'll see a picture of Tina Louise from Gilligan's Island)

Direction

- SPRINKLE gelatine over water in small bowl; stir to dissolve.
- Cool slightly.
- Pour evaporated milk into medium mixer bowl.
- Add gelatine and stir.
- Place bowl in freezer for about 30 - 40 minutes or until ice crystals form around edge of bowl
- BEAT cream cheese in medium bowl on high until light & fluffy
- Add marshmallow cream; beat until light & fluffy, set aside
- REMOVE chilled evaporated milk from freezer.
- Beat on high speed for 1 to 2 minutes or until stiff peaks form
- Slowly add powdered sugar and continue beating for 1 minute
- Add beaten cream cheese mixture to whipped milk; beat until blended.
- Stir in lime juice and lime zest
- Spoon into serving dishes; refrigerate at least 1 hour
- Sprinkle each serving with lime zest, if desired.
- Insert cookie into each mousse
- ***
- -No one can make you feel inferior without your consent-

- Eleanor Roosevelt
- ***
- One of my favourite sayings!!

---

109. Lemon Lime Mousse Recipe

Serving: 6 | Prep: | Cook: 12mins | Ready in:

Ingredients

- 6 tablespoons unsalted butter, room temperature
- 1 1/3 cups sugar
- 2 large eggs PLUS 2 egg yolks
- 1/2 cup fresh lemon juice
- 2 tablespoons fresh lime juice
- 1 teaspoon lemon zest PLUS more for garnish
- 1 1/2 cups heavy cream

Direction

- In a medium saucepan whisk together 1 cup sugar, eggs, yolks and lemon and lime juices (mixture may appear curdled).
- Place over low heat; cook, stirring until smooth, about 4 to 5 minutes.
- Raise heat to medium; cook stirring constantly until thick enough to coat the back of a spoon, 4 to 8 minutes.
- DO NOT BOIL!
- Remove pan from heat and stir in zest.
- Transfer mixture to a bowl.
- Cover surface of lemon curd with plastic wrap.
- Chill at least 1 hour.
- **The curd may stay refrigerated for up to 2 days before using.
- In a mixing bowl beat cream and remaining 1/3 cup sugar to soft peaks.
- Whisk lemon curd to loosen.
- Gently fold whipped cream into curd.
- Spoon into 6 glasses.
- Cover and chill at least 2 hours and up to 3 days.
- Just prior to serving, garnish with zest.

---

110. Lemon Mascarpone Mousse Recipe

Serving: 12 | Prep: | Cook: 5mins | Ready in:

Ingredients

- 2, 16 oz containers of mascarpone cheese
- 1 cup white granulated sugar or to taste
- 2 large lemons, juice from two, zest from one
- Optional : few drops of Fiori Di Silica- to make it even over the top

Direction

- Using an electric mixer, mix all medium speed till well blended thick and smooth.
- Use as is or as desired in dessert recipes
- Note: Fiori di sicilia is a flavour oil- combination of citrus and vanilla, available from King Arthur Baker's catalogue

---

111. Lemon Mousse Cake Recipe

Serving: 12 | Prep: | Cook: | Ready in:

Ingredients

- 2 packages (2.6 oz each) whipped topping mix
- 1 cup milk
- 1 package (3 oz) lemon jello
- 2/3 cup boiling water
- 1/2 cup ice cubes
- 2 packages soft ladyfingers
- 2 teaspoons lemon zest
- 4 drops yellow food coloring
- lemon jelly candies

Direction

- At medium high speed beat topping mix and milk until thickened; reserve.
- Stir jello mix into water until dissolved; stir in ice cubes until dissolved.
- At medium speed, slowly beat jello mixture into topping mixture until combined.
- At medium high speed beat until fluffy.
- Add lemon zest and food colouring; combine into mixture.
- Coat a 9 inch springform pan with cooking spray.
- Line pan with split soft ladyfingers, sides and bottom.
- Spoon mixture into springform pan.
- Cover with plastic; chill for 2 hours or until set.
- Top with whipped topping and lemon jelly candies.

112. Lemon Mousse Recipe

Serving: 0 | Prep: | Cook: 30mins | Ready in:

Ingredients

- • 4 medium free-range eggs, separated
- • 250g/8oz caster sugar
- • 3 lemons, zest and juice only
- • 5 tbsp cold water
- • 15g/½oz powdered gelatine
- • 300ml/½ pint double cream
- • small handful blanched toasted almonds, finely chopped

Direction

- Using an electric whisk, whisk together the egg yolks, sugar, lemon zest and juice until the sugar has dissolved and the mixture has thickened a little. (If you do not have an electric whisk, whisk by hand in a glass bowl set over a pan of hot water. When the mixture has thickened, remove the bowl from the pan and whisk until cool.)
- Place the cold water into a heavy-based saucepan, sprinkle in the gelatine and place over a gentle heat, without stirring, until the gelatine has melted. Remove from the heat and leave to cool slightly.
- In a separate bowl, lightly whip the cream until soft peaks form when the whisk is removed. Stir the melted gelatine into the cream and fold into the egg yolk mixture.
- Whisk the egg whites in a separate bowl with an electric hand-whisk until soft peaks form when the whisk is removed.
- Place the bowl with the egg yolks inside a bigger bowl filled with ice-cold water. Gently fold the whipped egg whites into the egg yolk mixture with a metal spoon. Stir the mixture until it begins to thicken, then pour into a glass bowl and refrigerate for one hour, or until set.
- Sprinkle the toasted chopped almonds over the top of the mousse and serve.

113. Lemon Mousse With Fresh Berries Recipe

Serving: 8 | Prep: | Cook: | Ready in:

Ingredients

- 1 cup plus 1 tablespoon sugar
- 3/4 cup fresh lemon juice
- 6 large organic egg yolks
- 2 large organic eggs
- 1 1/2 tablespoons grated lemon peel
- ~~~~~~~~~~~~~~~~~~~~~~~~~~~~~~
  ~~~~~~~~~~~~~~~~~~~
- 1 12-ounce basket strawberries, hulled, halved (or quartered if large)
- 1 6-ounce basket fresh blueberries
- 1 6-ounce basket fresh raspberries
- 1 6-ounce basket fresh blackberries
- ~~~~~~~~~~~~~~~~~~~~~~~~~~~~~~
  ~~~~~~~~~~~~~~~~~~~

- 2 cups chilled whipping cream
- ~~~~~~~~~~~~~~~~~~~~~~~~~~~~~~~~
- extra berries (for garnish)
- Fresh mint sprigs

Direction

- Combine 1 cup sugar, lemon juice, 6 egg yolks, 2 whole eggs and grated lemon peel in large metal bowl. Set bowl over saucepan of simmering water (do not allow bowl to touch water). Whisk until mixture thickens and thermometer inserted into mixture registers 160°F. Transfer lemon curd to another large bowl. Chill until cool, whisking occasionally.
- Toss halved strawberries, blueberries, raspberries, blackberries and remaining 1 tablespoon sugar in another large bowl.
- Using electric mixer, beat 1 1/2 cups cream in medium bowl until medium-firm peaks form. Fold 1/3 of whipped cream into lemon curd to lighten, then fold in remaining whipped cream.
- Divide berry mixture among 8 dessert bowls or wineglasses (or use disposable plastic tumblers). Spoon lemon mousse over berries. (Can be prepared 1 day ahead. Cover and refrigerate.)
- Using electric mixer, beat remaining 1/2 cup cream in medium bowl until stiff peaks form. Spoon whipped cream atop desserts or transfer whipped cream to pastry bag fitted with large star tip and pipe atop desserts. Garnish with berries and mint sprigs.

114. Lemon Mousse With Fresh Berries Recipe

Serving: 8 | Prep: | Cook: 15mins | Ready in:

Ingredients

- 1 cup plus 1 tablespoon sugar
- 3/4 cup fresh lemon juice
- 6 large egg yolks
- 2 large eggs
- 1 1/2 tablespoons grated lemon peel
- 1 12-ounce basket strawberries, hulled, halved (or quartered if large)
- 1 6-ounce basket fresh blueberries
- 1 6-ounce basket fresh raspberries
- 1 6-ounce basket fresh blackberries
- 2 cups chilled whipping cream
- 8 whole strawberries (for garnish)
- Fresh mint sprigs

Direction

- Combine 1 cup sugar, lemon juice, 6 egg yolks, 2 whole eggs and grated lemon peel in large metal bowl. Set bowl over saucepan of simmering water (do not allow bowl to touch water). Whisk until mixture thickens and thermometer inserted into mixture registers 160°F. Transfer lemon curd to another large bowl. Chill until cool, whisking occasionally.
- Toss halved strawberries, blueberries, raspberries, blackberries and remaining 1 tablespoon sugar in another large bowl.
- Using electric mixer, beat 1 1/2 cups cream in medium bowl until medium-firm peaks form. Fold 1/3 of whipped cream into lemon curd to lighten, then fold in remaining whipped cream.
- Divide berry mixture among 8 dessert bowls or wineglasses. Spoon lemon mousse over berries. (Can be prepared 1 day ahead. Cover and refrigerate.)
- Using electric mixer, beat remaining 1/2 cup cream in medium bowl until stiff peaks form. Spoon whipped cream atop desserts or transfer whipped cream to pastry bag fitted with large star tip and pipe atop desserts. Garnish with whole strawberries and mint sprigs.

115. Lemon And Cocoa Mousse Recipe

Serving: 6 | Prep: | Cook: 120mins | Ready in:

Ingredients

- FOR THE MOUSSE
- 1 can condensed milk
- 1 can evaporated milk
- 1/2 cup lemon juice
- 2 tsp. grated lemon peel
- DECORATION
- 1 tbsp. sifted unsweetened cocoa

Direction

- FOR THE MOUSSE
- 1. Take the evaporated milk out of the can, put it in a bowl and freeze for 2 hours.
- 2. Take out from freezer and mix with electric mixer at medium speed until soft peaks form.
- 3. Add condensed milk and continue mixing.
- 4. Add lemon juice.
- 5. Mix, when all the ingredients are well incorporated pour in a pretty bowl.
- DECORATION
- Sift unsweetened cocoa.
- You may serve it with chocolate cookies.
- Enjoy!

116. Lemon And White Chocolate Mousse Parfaits With Strawberries Recipe

Serving: 8 | Prep: | Cook: 20mins | Ready in:

Ingredients

- 5 large egg yolks
- 1/2 cup sugar
- 1/2 cup fresh lemon juice
- 4 teaspoons finely grated lemon peel
- Pinch of salt
- 1/4 cup plus 2 2/3 cups chilled heavy whipping cream
- 1 3.5-ounce bar high-quality white chocolate (such as Lindt or Perugina), finely chopped
- 5 cups sliced hulled strawberries (about 2 pounds)

Direction

- Whisk egg yolks, sugar, lemon juice, lemon peel, and salt in medium metal bowl to blend.
- Set bowl over saucepan of simmering water.
- Whisk until mixture is very thick and thermometer inserted into centre registers 160°F to 170°F, about 6 minutes.
- Remove bowl from over water. Cool lemon mousse base to room temperature.
- Combine 1/4 cup cream and white chocolate in another medium metal bowl. Set bowl over saucepan of barely simmering water.
- Stir constantly until chocolate is soft and almost melted.
- Remove bowl from over water and stir until white chocolate is melted and smooth.
- Cool white chocolate mousse base to room temperature.
- Beat remaining 2 2/3 cups cream in large bowl until firm peaks form.
- Divide whipped cream between both mousse bases, folding in 1 cup at a time (about 3 cups for each).
- Layer scant 1/4 cup lemon mousse in each of 8 parfait glasses or wineglasses; top with 2 tablespoons strawberries.
- Layer scant 1/4 cup white chocolate mousse over strawberries. Repeat layering 1 more time. DO AHEAD: Can be made 1 day ahead.
- Cover with plastic wrap and chill. Cover and chill remaining strawberries.
- Spoon strawberries over top of each parfait, if desired, and serve.

117. Light Chocolate Mousse Recipe

Serving: 6 | Prep: | Cook: 20mins | Ready in:

Ingredients

- 1/2c boiling water
- 2tsp gelatin powder
- 1 1/2Tbs cocoa powder
- 4 eggs, seperated
- 1/3c superfine sugar
- 1 pinch cream of tarter

Direction

- Combine water and gelatine in a jug. Whisk with a fork till gelatine has been dissolved
- Stir cocoa into the gelatine mix. Set aside to cool for 10 mins.
- In large mixer bowl, beat egg whites and cream of tartar till soft peaks form. Slowly add the sugar and beat till thick and glossy (beat between slow additions of sugar). With mixer on high speed, add egg yolks, one at a time.
- Slowly pour gelatine mixture into egg mixture. Beat constantly till well combined.
- Pour mixture into 6 serving cups and refrigerate for 4 hours or till set.
- Dust with some extra cocoa to serve or use some chocolate shavings.

118. Light Strawberry Mousse Recipe

Serving: 4 | Prep: | Cook: | Ready in:

Ingredients

- 1/2 cup 35% cream (liquid)
- 2 cups fresh strawberries (you may also use other berries if you prefer)
- 1 egg white
- 1 pinch of salt
- 4 tablespoons of white sugar or 3 tablespoons of splenda or other sugar substitute

Direction

- Whip the 35% cream to form stiff peaks.
- Remove the stems from the strawberries and wash. Mash the strawberries well.
- Whip the egg white with a hand mixer until it becomes stiff peaks, add the salt. Continue whipping while adding small quantities of the sugar (or splenda) a little at a time until well incorporated and shiny.
- Fold in the strawberries in the egg white and then the whipped cream gently.
- Pour the mousse into serving bowls and refrigerate 2 hours before serving. Garnish with a fresh strawberry on each serving and serve.

119. Lime Mango Mousse In Chocolate Cups Recipe

Serving: 8 | Prep: | Cook: | Ready in:

Ingredients

- 6 oz. white or bittersweet chocolate
- 2 cups prepared whipped cream
- 1 tsp. grated lime rind
- 1 tbsp. lime juice
- 1/2 cup powdered sugar
- 1 peeled & pureed mango
- 1 (250g.) pkg. cream cheese

Direction

- To make chocolate cups: melt 6 oz. white or bittersweet chocolate. Using a small spoon, lightly coat the inside of 8 foil-lined baking cups. Freeze for 10 minutes. Recoat any thin spots and freeze 1 hour.
- In an electric mixer, at medium speed, beat 1 pkg.(250g) Cream Cheese with 1 peeled, pureed mango,1/2 cup powdered sugar, 1

tbsp. fresh lime juice and 1 tsp. grated lime rind until smooth. Fold in 2 cups prepared DREAM WHIP. Spoon into chocolate cups and refrigerate.

120. Lime Mousse Recipe

Serving: 6 | Prep: | Cook: 1hours10mins | Ready in:

Ingredients

- 2 cups double cream
- 1 can condensed milk
- 6 gelatin sheets, soaked in water
- juice of 4 limes
- zest of one lime

Direction

- Put the cream, condensed milk and juice of 4 limes on a blender or food processor and whizz.
- Melt the gelatine with 2 tbsp. water in a small sauce pan over low heat. Do NOT let it boil!! It will make the mousse bitter.
- Blend the melted gelatine into the mousse and blend.
- Pour on a nice serving bowl and put it in the freezer for at least 1 hour.
- Before serving sprinkle the zest of 1 lime on top.

121. Low Fat Dark Chocolate Mousse Recipe

Serving: 4 | Prep: | Cook: 30mins | Ready in:

Ingredients

- 50 g sugar
- 2 eggs
- 200 g Dark baking chocolate, chopped
- 100 ml whip cream
- 400 ml Low Fat Plain vanilla yogurt
- 1 tsp gelatine in 1 1/2 tbsp hot water
- fresh fruits - 3 strawberries, 3 red seedless grapes, a Slice of apricot
- 1 tsp icing sugar

Direction

- Heat the Whip Cream. Remove before it starts to bubble.
- Add the chocolate. Stir until melted.
- Cool it completely.
- Whisk the Eggs and Sugar until white and fluffy.
- Fold in the Melted Chocolate.
- Gently fold in the Yogurt.
- Mix the Gelatine.
- Pour in a disposable mould (OR in serving cups and chill to set for at least 2 to 3 hrs.).
- Refrigerate
- Once it's almost starts to set, turn it upside down and chill overnight.
- Top it with some fresh fruits and Icing sugar.
- Decorate using your imagination.
- ALWAYS KEEP CHILLED and MUST CONSUME WITHIN 24 HRS.

122. Low Fat Oreo Mousse Recipe

Serving: 6 | Prep: | Cook: | Ready in:

Ingredients

- 1 (1.5 ounce) sugar fee chocolate instant pudding mix-dry
- 1 (12 ounce) Cool Whip Free
- 4 reduced fat Oreos-crushed

Direction

- Mix pudding and cool whip free together for about 2 minutes by hand (with spatula) until well mixed. Stir in cookie crumbs, reserving about 1 crumbled cookie to sprinkle on top.

- Put into individual dessert cups. (If you don't have dessert cups, wide mouth wine glasses work great)
- Serve chilled

123. Lusciously Rich Chocolate Pie Recipe

Serving: 0 | Prep: | Cook: 1hours | Ready in:

Ingredients

- CRUST
- 1 cup dates (seeded)
- 1 cup finely chopped walnuts
- 1 cup hazelnut/almond meal
- ....
- FILLING
- 1 cup macadamia milk
- ½ cup maple syrup
- 1 cup chia seeds
- 2 tbsp cacao powder
- 1 tbsp stevia
- Pinch of sea salt
- ....
- TOPPING
- 1-2 avocados
- ½ cup maple syrup
- 1 tbsp cacao powder
- 1 tsp stevia

Direction

- CRUST
- Mash the dates with the chopped walnuts.
- Use the hazelnut meal to thicken mix.
- Line a pie dish with baking paper.
- Put mix into pie dish as a crust/base for the pie.
- FILLING
- Blend all ingredients together.
- Let sit for 15 minutes. Blend again.
- Sit for another 15 mins then blend again.
- TOPPING
- Blend all ingredients together.
- Chill each section of pie separately.
- Assemble pie just before serving.
- Pour chia seed mix into pie crust.
- Smooth out.
- Spread over the avocado topping.
- Pop in freezer for 30 minutes.
- Serve with some fresh or frozen berries
- Can be served with freshly whipped cream and a dusting of chocolate.

124. Mango Berry And Lemon Mousse Dessert Recipe

Serving: 24 | Prep: | Cook: 60mins | Ready in:

Ingredients

- 1 cup boiling water
- 2 pkg. (4-serving size each) jell-o brand lemon flavor gelatin
- 1 cup sour cream
- 1 sleeve crackers (30 crackers), finely crushed
- 1/4 cup sugar
- 1/4 cup (1/2 stick) butter or margarine, melted
- 2-1/2 cups thawed Cool Whip whipped topping, divided
- 1 large mango, peeled, pitted and chopped
- 1-1/4 cups fresh raspberries

Direction

- STIR boiling water into dry gelatine mixes in large bowl at least 2 min. until completely dissolved; pour into blender. Add sour cream; blend until smooth. Pour into large bowl; cover. Refrigerate 15 min. or until cooled. Meanwhile, mix cracker crumbs, sugar and butter. Press onto bottom of 13x9-inch pan.
- ADD 2 cups of the whipped topping to gelatine mixture; stir with wire whisk until well blended. Spread over crust; top with fruit. Refrigerate 30 min. or until firm.

- SERVE topped with dollops of the remaining 1/2 cup whipped topping. Store leftovers in refrigerator.

125. Mango Mousse Recipe

Serving: 6 | Prep: | Cook: 60mins | Ready in:

Ingredients

- 1 fourteen-oz. can sweetened condensed milk
- 1 1/2 to 2 lbs ripe mango, peeled seeded and cut in chunks
- 2T lime juice
- 1 c chilled heavy (whipping) cream
- sliced bananas or strawberries (optional)

Direction

- Puree mangoes, condensed milk and lime juice in a blender until smooth.
- Whip cream until almost stiff; fold it gently into the mango puree.
- Pour into individual serving dishes, or one large dish.
- Chill for at least one hour, or more.
- Top with a dollop of whipped cream and sliced bananas or strawberries, if desired.

126. Mango And Orange Mousse Recipe

Serving: 4 | Prep: | Cook: 45mins | Ready in:

Ingredients

- 2 large ripe mangos
- ¼ cup fresh orange juice
- finely grated zest of 1 orange
- ¼ cup superfine sugar
- 2 tsp unflavored gelatin powder
- pinch of salt
- 1 large egg white
- 2/3 cup heavy cream

Direction

- Cut the flesh off both sides of the mango stone. Scoop out the flesh and discard the skin. Set aside 1 piece of mango.
- Cut the remaining mango, including the flesh clinging to the stone, into chunks.
- Puree with the orange juice in a food processor.
- Transfer to a bowl and stir in the orange zest and superfine sugar.
- Sprinkle the gelatine over 3 tbsp. water in a small heatproof bowl and let stand for 5 minutes until softened.
- Place the bowl in a saucepan of gently simmering water and stir until the gelatine has completely dissolved.
- Cool slightly, then stir into the mango puree.
- Whip the egg white and salt in a large, clean bowl until stiff peaks form.
- Fold the egg white mixture into the mango mixture.
- Whip the cream to soft peaks.
- Fold half into the mango mixture. Divide the mixture among 4 dessert glasses.
- Refrigerate until the mousses are set, at least 1 hour or up to 2 days.
- Slice the reserved mango.
- Top each serving with a dollop of whipped cream and a mango slice. Serve chilled.

127. Maple Nut Mousse Pie Recipe

Serving: 8 | Prep: | Cook: | Ready in:

Ingredients

- 3/4 cup pure maple syrup
- 3 eggs separated
- 1 cup choped walnuts
- chocolate cookie crumb pie shell
- dash salt

- 2 cups whipped topping
- 2 tbs shaved choclate

Direction

- Beat yolks bright yellow in colour.
- Add maple syrup and salt.
- Cook in double boiler till mixtures thicken
- Cool
- Beat whites stiff.
- Fold into cooled mixture with 2/3rds of whipped topping together.
- Pour into shell.
- Cover with remaining topping
- Sprinkle with chocolate
- Freeze at least 4 hours

128. Midnight Mousse Recipe

Serving: 2 | Prep: | Cook: 5mins | Ready in:

Ingredients

- 2- tablespoons sugar ....
- 1/2 -teaspoon unflavored gelatin .....
- 1/4 -cup milk .....
- 1/2- cup HERSHEY'S SPECIAL dark chocolate chips ....
- 1 -tablespoon raspberry-flavored liqueur ....(i like the liqueur like chambord .)......(or 1 teaspoon vanilla extract)........
- 1/2- cup cold whipping cream ...
- sweetened whipped cream.
- fresh raspberries......

Direction

- Stir together sugar and gelatine in small saucepan; stir in milk. Let stand 2 minutes to soften gelatine.
- Cook over medium heat, stirring constantly, until mixture just begins to boil.
- Remove from heat. Immediately add chocolate chips; stir until melted.
- Stir in liqueur; cool to room temperature.
- Beat whipping cream in small bowl until stiff; gradually add chocolate mixture, folding gently just until blended.
- Spoon into serving dishes.
- Refrigerate.
- Garnish with sweetened whipped cream and raspberries, if desired. 2 servings.
- _____

- VARIATION: For high-standing mousse,
- Prepare collars for 2 parfait glasses.
- Tear strip of foil of sufficient length to go around top of each glass. Fold foil into fourths; butter lightly.
- Place buttered side in; tape to sides of glasses.
- Spoon mousse into glasses. (Mousse should come over top of glasses.) After mousse has set, carefully remove foil collar.

129. Milk Chocolate Coffee Mousse In A Cocoa Nib Florentina Cup Recipe

Serving: 12 | Prep: | Cook: 10mins | Ready in:

Ingredients

- milk chocolate coffee Mousse:
- 3 cups heavy cream
- 6 egg yolks 1/3 cup honey
- 1/4 cup coffee liqueur
- 10 oz milk chocolate (0.63 lb)
- 4 oz sweet dark chocolate (0.25 lb)
- cocoa Nib Florentina Cups:
- 7 oz unsalted butter (0.44 lb)
- 10 oz sugar (0.63 lb)
- 3 oz honey (0.19 lb)
- 3 oz heavy cream (0.19 lb)
- 12 oz sliced almonds (0.75 lb)
- 2 oz finely ground almonds or hazelnuts (0.13 lb)
- 2 oz bread flour (0.13 lb)

Direction

- For the mousse. Whip the heavy cream to soft peaks and set aside
- Whip the egg yolks to ribbon stage
- Heat the honey until it starts to boil and quickly whip it into the egg yolks until the egg mixture is fluffy and no longer warm
- Stir in the coffee liqueur.
- Melt the both of the chocolate in a double boiler until melted.
- Incorporate the warm chocolate into the egg yolk mixture.
- Fold the heavy cream into the egg yolk mixture.
- For the Florentina cups. Boil the butter, sugar, honey, and heavy cream until it has reached a temperature of 240. Do not over stir this mixture, it will crystalize if you do.
- Once it has hit a temperature of 240. Crush the sliced almonds in your hand and add it into the mixture.
- Also add in you ground almonds or hazelnuts, cocoa nib, and bread flour and mix together.
- Use a tablespoon to scoop the florentina batter on to a silpat and mash it flat to get a circle. Bake at 375F until brown.
- When removing the florentina cups off the silpat let it rest until it is ready to be pliable and will not fall apart. Use a metal spatula to get the florentina off and mould over a ladle or bowl. If the florentina has fully set you can return it to the oven to let it melt down again and mould.
- After you have shaped the cups take the mousse and pipe it into the cups. And you can make whip cream to top off the chocolate coffee mousse.

130. Mimi's Chocolate Mousse Recipe

Serving: 18 | Prep: | Cook: 3hours | Ready in:

Ingredients

- 8 ounces semi-sweet Valrhona dark chocolate
- 6 large eggs, separate yolks and eggs
- 3 Tablespoons water
- 1/4 cup Grand Marnier (2 oz)
- 4 cups heavy whipping cream (divide into two 2-cup portions)
- 6 Tablespoons sugar (divide into 2 and 4 Tablespoons)
- 1 cup powdered sugar

Direction

- For Chocolate
- Under low heat, use a double boiler to melt chocolate pieces. Set aside.
- For Egg Yolks
- In a heavy sauce pan on very low heat, Vigorously whisk egg yolks and water continuously until yolks begin to foam, add Grand Marnier. Continue to whisk until thickens enough to coat back of spoon (such as hollandaise). Be careful to not cook egg yolks. Pour sauce through strainer and discard solids. Combine chocolate and egg mixture in large bowl and fold together. Set aside.
- Whipped Cream
- Using stand mixer with balloon whisk, beat 2 cups heavy whipping cream on high 2-3 minutes until stiff peaks form. Add 2 Tablespoons sugar. Fold into chocolate/egg mixture.
- Meringue
- Using stand mixer with balloon whisk, whisk egg whites on high until soft peaks form for about 1-2 minutes, Add 4 Tablespoons sugar and continue to beat until stiff peaks form, approximately 2-3 minutes. Add to chocolate mixture.
- Serving Portions
- Spoon into serving cups and chill until ready to serve. Garnish with whipped cream piped on top and dust with chocolate shavings.
- Enjoy!

131. Mocha Marshmallow Mousse Recipe

Serving: 6 | Prep: | Cook: 20mins | Ready in:

Ingredients

- 2 (3.5-oz) milk chocolate bars; broken
- 20 larges White marshmallows
- ⅓ cup milk
- 2 teaspoons instant coffee granules
- 2 Egg whites; beaten
- 1 cup Whipping cream; whipped
- Almonds; sliced and unsalted
- Additional whipped cream (optional)

Direction

- Heat chocolate bars, marshmallows, milk and coffee in a double boiler until melted, stirring occasionally.
- Remove from heat and cool.
- Fold in beaten egg whites and whipped cream.
- Pour into a 5 cup mould or individual cups.
- Refrigerate or freeze, good served either way.
- When serving, sprinkle with sliced almonds, or whipped cream, if desired.
- Yield: 6 to 8 servings.
- Credits:
- JENNY BOSHEARS (MRS. BARRY) From , by the Little Rock (AR) Junior League. Downloaded from Glen's MM Recipe Archive.

132. Mocha Tortoni MOUSSE Recipe

Serving: 8 | Prep: | Cook: | Ready in:

Ingredients

- 2 large egg whites
- 2 tbsp instant coffee
- pinch of salt
- 1/4 cup sugar
- 2 cups whipping cream
- 2tsp vanilla
- 1/2 cup sugar
- 1/4 cup toiasted almonds
- 2 oz grated chocolate, grated

Direction

- In a medium bowl, beat egg whites until foamy.
- Add coffee crystals and salt and beat until well combined.
- Gradually add 1/4 cup sugar and beat until soft peaks form.
- Set aside (in fridge)
- In a separate bowl, whip cream until soft peaks form.
- Beat in vanilla and 1/2 cup sugar.
- Fold both bowls together and mix gently
- Fold in almonds and transfer to a large glass bowl and freeze at least 2 hours.
- Garnish with grated chocolate.

133. Mom's Cherry Cheesecake Recipe

Serving: 8 | Prep: | Cook: 2hours | Ready in:

Ingredients

- Topping:
- 2 c. cherries
- 6 tbsp. sugar
- 3 tbsp. cornstarch
- 1/4 tsp. red food color
- 1/4 tsp. almond flavor
- 1 tbsp. lemon juice
- Crust:
- 2 c. graham cracker crumbs
- 1/4 c. sugar
- 1/4 c. butter
- cheese Filling:
- 1 2/3 c. evaporated milk or whipping cream
- 3 tbsp. lemon juice
- 1 pkg. unflavored gelatin

- 3 tbsp. cold water
- 3 oz. cream cheese
- 1 c. powdered sugar

Direction

- For the topping, mix all together and boil until slightly thickened. Cool.
- For the crust, melt butter in pie pan or 8x8 pan, mix crackers and sugar in with it, and press in bottom of pan.
- For the filling, soften gelatine in cold water. Stir until dissolved OVER hot water, do not add hot water to it! Let cool. Have evaporated milk chilled, whip until stiff. Add lemon juice and blend. Blend sugar and softened cream cheese, then add gelatine. Fold with whipped milk or cream. Pour into crust. Allow to set for at least 10 minutes. Spread cherry topping over all, and chill.

134. Mothers Day Chocolate Mousse With Sauce Recipe

Serving: 6 | Prep: | Cook: 240mins | Ready in:

Ingredients

- 3/4 cup raspberry jam
- 1 Tbsp. raspberry liqueur or orange juice
- 3 oz. semisweet chocolate
- 1 oz. bittersweet chocolate
- 2 Tbsp. honey
- 1 Tbsp. brandy or orange juice
- 2-1/2 cups whipping cream
- chocolate curls or grated chocolate

Direction

- In a small saucepan heat the jam over low heat until melted, stirring occasionally. Remove from heat. Stir in raspberry liqueur or orange juice; set aside to cool completely.
- In another small saucepan heat chocolates over low heat until melted and smooth. Remove from heat. Stir in the honey, brandy or orange juice, and 1 tablespoon of the whipping cream until well combined. Transfer mixture to a large bowl and set aside to cool completely.
- In a chilled, large mixing bowl beat the remaining whipping cream until stiff peaks just form. Remove 1 cup of the whipped cream and set aside. Stir 1/2 cup of the whipping cream into the chocolate mixture to lighten. Fold remaining whipped cream into the cooled chocolate mixture.
- Spoon the chocolate mixture into 6 stemmed wine glasses or dessert dishes. Top with reserved whipped cream. Spoon cooled raspberry sauce over and top with chocolate curls. Cover and chill for 1 to 6 hours. Makes 6 servings.
- Tip: For chocolate curls, slowly draw a vegetable peeler across the edge of a bar of semisweet or milk chocolate. It works best if chocolate is at room temperature.

135. Mothers Day Nutella Mousse Recipe

Serving: 6 | Prep: | Cook: 10mins | Ready in:

Ingredients

- 1 jar of nutella (chocolate hazelnut spread)
- 8 oz cream cheese softened to room temperature
- 8 oz heavy cream

Direction

- Beat the heavy cream to soft peaks
- Beat the Nutella and cream cheese to blend well
- Blend the whipped cream into the Nutella cream cheese mixture.
- At this point it can be served immediately as it remains fluffy
- Chill if desired for a firmer consistency.

- No matter how you serve it is quite delicious!
- Notes: serve mousse with a dollop of whipped cream if desired
- Also one can add a bit of liqueur or brewed cooled espresso to give it an added flavour if desired

136. Mousse Berry Shells Recipe

Serving: 6 | Prep: | Cook: 3hours | Ready in:

Ingredients

- For Mousse
- 3oz white baking chocolate(not "candy coating"), cut into 1/2 inch pieces
- 3/4 cup whipping cream
- 1t vanilla
- For honey lemon Glazed Berries
- 1 cup mixed fresh berries(blueberries, blackberries, raspberries, strawberries, etc)
- 2T honey
- 2T fresh lemon juice
- For Pastries
- 1 package(6 ct) puff pastry shells, frozen

Direction

- For Mousse
- In small saucepan, or microwave, melt chocolate and 1/4 cream using low heat and stirring often. This should only take about 5 minutes, on the stove top.
- Add vanilla and stir to combine.
- Set aside to cool completely
- When cool, begin whipping remaining cream with hand or stand mixer, to create stiff peaks.
- Carefully fold in cooled white chocolate
- Refrigerate at least 1 hour.
- Honey Lemon Glazed Berries
- In small sauce pan, heat lemon juice and honey, over low heat.
- Stir to combine and cook until warmed through.
- Remove from heat and carefully fold in berries to coat
- Set aside to cool completely.
- Puff Pastry
- Prepare shells per package directions, remove tops, and let shells cool.
- To assemble, spoon mousse into shells and top with berries. Remove berries from glaze with slotted spoon, if needed.

137. Mousse Chocolat With A Dash Of Cinnamon And Rum Recipe

Serving: 12 | Prep: | Cook: | Ready in:

Ingredients

- 50 gram sugar
- 1 teaspoon cinnamon
- 3 spoons of dark rum
- 3 eggs
- 250 gram cream
- 250 gram dark chocolate (Belgian)

Direction

- Melt the chocolate "au bain-marie"
- Whip the cream
- Separate the eggs white and yellow
- Beat the eggs white until you can hold the bowl upside down. The egg white should stay in :-)
- In a large bowl with a hand held mixer, place the sugar and the egg yellow, and cream together until light and fluffy.
- Add the teaspoon of cinnamon and the spoons of rum and stir
- Add the whipped cream and stir
- Add the beaten egg whites and gently stir it under.
- Put in the refrigerator for at least 3 hours.
- Bon Appetit!

138. Mousse Chocolate Tart Recipe

Serving: 8 | Prep: | Cook: 20mins | Ready in:

Ingredients

- 215 gr chocolate cookies crumbled.
- 1 egg white,
- 1 tbs honey.
- 2 ts gelatine powder.
- 225 gr confectionery sugar.
- 1 c cocao powder.
- 80 gr luke warm milk.
- 1 ts vanilla flavour.
- 1 1/2 c heavy cream.
- 85 gr cooking chocolate.

Direction

- Butter a non-stick flat baking tin 25 cm diameter, preheat the oven to 180 degrees.
- Mix cookies, egg white and honey till you have a dough and push in the baking tin also up to the sides, put in the oven and bake 15 min, set aside and let cool.
- In a small saucepan put 3 tbsp. water and the gelatine, warm on low heat for 2 min, stir till gelatine is dissolved and take of the heat.
- In a big bowl mix sugar and cacao, add milk and vanilla and mix well, add gelatine, mix well and let cool down.
- Beat heavy cream till smooth and firm and add 3/4 of cold cocoa mixture and softly stir.
- Put cream cacao mixture in tart base top with the rest of heavy cream in the middle.
- Refrigerate overnight, next day sprinkle with cacao powder and chocolate curls, (cut the chocolate sidewise with a peeler) and serve.

139. Mousse Chokolat Recipe

Serving: 6 | Prep: | Cook: 10mins | Ready in:

Ingredients

- 1/2 lb of bakers chocolate
- 1/4 cup whole milk or half and half
- 5 large eggs, separated.
- 1 tsp vanilla
- 1 tbsp brandy
- 1/4 tsp orange zest
- About 30 raspberries (Optional)

Direction

- In the top of a double boiler melt the chocolate and mix in the milk.
- Add the yolks of the eggs, vanilla, cinnamon, orange zest and brandy. Stir until blended and smooth. Set aside.
- Beat the whites of the eggs until peaks form. Add a little sugar if desired.
- Fill small bowls or glasses about 1/2 inch from the top with the chocolate mousse. Top with whipped cream and (optional) add berries.
- Cool in refrigerator about 1/2 hour or longer.

140. Mousse Au Chocolat Recipe

Serving: 8 | Prep: | Cook: | Ready in:

Ingredients

- 8 ounces bittersweet or semisweet chocolate, chopped
- 4 tablespoons unsalted butter
- 3 large eggs, separated
- 1/4 cup super fine sugar
- 1 1/4 cups cold heavy cream
- 1/4 cup Grand Marnier
- Small chocolate shavings or chocolate nibs, for garnish

Direction

- In the top of a double boiler or in a bowl set over a pot of hot water, melt the chocolate and

butter, stirring. Remove from the heat and beat with a heavy wooden spoon until smooth. Return to the heat and 1 at a time, add the yolks, beating well after the addition of each. Remove from the heat and transfer to a large bowl.
- In a clean bowl, beat the egg whites until soft peaks start to form. Add 2 tablespoons of the sugar and beat until stiff.
- In a third bowl, beat the cream until it becomes frothy. Add the remaining 2 tablespoons sugar and the Grand Marnier and continue beating until it holds soft peaks.
- Fold the egg whites into the chocolate mixture until no white speaks appear. Gradually fold in the whipped cream, reserving about 1/2 cup for garnish.
- Transfer to a large decorative silver or glass bowl and refrigerate until well chilled.
- To serve, spoon the reserved whipped cream on top and garnish with chocolate shavings.

141. My Chocolate Mousse Recipe

Serving: 4 | Prep: | Cook: 6mins | Ready in:

Ingredients

- milk-3 cups
- Fresh heavy cream-1/2 cup
- eggs-2
- gelatine-2tbsp
- cocoa powder-4tbsp
- sugar-2 cups(or acc. to taste)
- almond essence-few drops
- Silvers of almonds- garnish

Direction

- Mix gelatine in 1/2 cup cold water, set aside
- Beat eggs, till light and frothy.
- Heat milk in a saucepan, add eggs, and keep stirring on low flame.
- Make a paste with cocoa and a little water in a cup, add this to the milk, and keep stirring.
- Add the cream and sugar.
- When the back of the spoon gets coated, then the custard gets ready.
- Add a few drops of almond essence.
- Heat up the gelatine on low fire until completely melted and clear.
- Add gelatine to cold custard.
- Cool completely, pour into wet mould and refrigerate.
- Serve chilled. Garnish with silvers of almonds.

142. No Cook Faux Chocolate Or Cinnamon Or Cappuccino Mousse Recipe

Serving: 6 | Prep: | Cook: 15mins | Ready in:

Ingredients

- 1 large container of Cool Whip or store brand non dairy whipped cream
- 2 packages of your favorite chocolate instant pudding mix (the darker the chocolate the better and try not to use milk chocolate it's too light in flavor)
- Your favorite chocolate syrup (hersheys, bosco etc)
- cinnamon, shaved chocolate and mint leaf for garnish (optional)

Direction

- Make the 2 packages of instant pudding according to the directions
- Add the entire container of cool whip
- Beat on high till mixed (yes you can use an electric mixer)
- Add the chocolate syrup and beat until you reach the desired density of the flavour of chocolate you want. The more syrup the deeper the flavour
- Chill for 15 minutes (if you can wait that long)

- Garnish with shaved chocolate and mint leaf or cinnamon if desired
- Believe it or not it is really not overly sweet.
- For a variation use a cappuccino pudding and cappuccino flavored syrup for a cappuccino mouse.

143. No Bake Nutella Cheesecake Recipe

Serving: 6 | Prep: | Cook: 1hours | Ready in:

Ingredients

- 2/3 cup nutella
- 8 oz Nuefchatel cheese
- 16 oz Cool Whip prepared topping (divided)
- 3 tablespoons powdered sugar
- 2 oz Frangelico (optional)
- 12 Oreo cookies
- hazelnuts, toasted
- chocolate, for garnish

Direction

- Place Oreo cookies in a food processor and pulse into fine crumbs. Spoon crumbs into the bottom of rocks or martini glass. Even out the crumbs and lightly press into the glass.
- In a mixing bowl combine Nutella, Neufchatel cheese, 8 ounces of whipped topping, and Frangelico. Whisk into a smooth creamy consistency and pipe into glasses on top of cookie layer.
- Whisk together 8 ounces of whipped topping with the powdered sugar (adding powdered sugar helps to keep the topping stiff). Pipe the whipped topping on to the Nutella layer.
- For my garnish I made some chocolate designs out of Wilton's Candy Melts. I use a square of granite that I freeze for about 4 hours (mine was a scrap from my counter tops, but you can get a square of marble or granite at a tile store). Temper the chocolate in the microwave and pour into small a piping bag. Pipe the chocolate directly onto the frozen stone.
- The chocolate will set up almost immediately. Using a pastry knife, metal spatula, or I use a putty knife that I reserve just for chocolates, transfer the designs onto wax paper and allow them to completely set up.
- Complete the dessert with the candy design and some toasted hazelnuts. (While the chocolate designs are easy to make you could also use a curl of chocolate, sprinkles, or a Ferro Wafer Roll).

144. Nutella Mousse Recipe

Serving: 6 | Prep: | Cook: 120mins | Ready in:

Ingredients

- 1.5 cups heavy whipping cream
- 1/2 cup nutella
- 2 tb. hot water
- 2 tsp. instant espresso or instant coffee
- 1 nipper hazelnut flavored Kahlua

Direction

- Dissolve instant espresso in hot water in small bowl. Add Nutella and Kahlua, beating until smooth. Put aside.
- Whip heavy cream until doubled in volume and it forms stiff peaks (Tip: chill the bowl and beaters to get a better whipped cream).
- Give Nutella mix a quick beat, and fold into whipped cream. Put into dessert glasses and chill 2 hours.
- Serves 4-6, depending on the serving.
- Top with a dollop of whipped cream and some sifted cocoa before serving.

145. ORANGE CHOCOLATE MOUSSE Recipe

Serving: 4 | Prep: | Cook: 10mins | Ready in:

Ingredients

- 2 eggs beaten
- 2 yolks beaten
- 1 cup heavy whipping cream
- 1/4 cup packed brown sugar
- 3 tbsp orange juice
- 1 1/2 tsp grated orange zest
- 6 squares semi-sweet chocolate, melted & cooled

Direction

- In a pot combine eggs, yolks, cream, brown sugar, juice and zest until blended.
- Cook and stir over medium low heat or until mixture is thickened. Remove from heat and stir in melted chocolate until smooth.
- Pour into desert dishes.
- Refrigerate at least 2 hours.

146. OREO CHOCOLATE MOUSSE Recipe

Serving: 6 | Prep: | Cook: 1mins | Ready in:

Ingredients

- 1 tin caramel treat----if u dont have place a can of unopened condensed milk in a pot of water..........boil for +_ 3hrs {add water all the time the can should be completely covered
- 3-4 Tabs cocoa powder
- 250 ml fresh cream
- 1 box oreos
- 1 box oreos

Direction

- Beat the caramel treat
- Add the cocoa to the caramel treat.....mixing well
- Whip cream until thick
- Fold the whipped cream into the caramel mixture
- Break the Oreos into quarters ....fold in
- Place into individual bowls / large pretty glass bowl
- Decorate with piped cream rosettes, whisper chocolates and a dusting of edible gold/bronze dust.......PUT ON THE CALORIES, DEARS.............LOL..............:] enjoy ...anyways...I did!!!

147. Orange And Almond Mousse Recipe

Serving: 0 | Prep: | Cook: 70mins | Ready in:

Ingredients

- 1 can Eagle Brand sweetened condensed milk
- 1/3 cup lemon juice
- 1/4 cup sliced almonds
- grated orange rind from one medium navel orange
- 1 cup whipping cream

Direction

- In large bowl blend Eagle Brand Milk and lemon juice, stirring until mixture thickens.
- Add the almonds and the grated orange rind.
- In a second bowl whip cream until stiff peaks form. Reserve 1/2 cup of the whipping cream for garnish.
- Fold the remainder into the Eagle Brand mixture.
- Pour into dishes and refrigerate for at least an hour.
- Garnish with whipped cream. I sometimes also put a couple of the sliced almonds on the top or as was the case last night, a slice of Terry's Chocolate Orange! :)

148. Oreo Cookie Desert Recipe

Serving: 8 | Prep: | Cook: 20mins | Ready in:

Ingredients

- 1-16 ounce package Oreo or Oreo type cookie
- 1-8 ounce cream cheese, thawed
- 1-15 ounce sweetened condensed milk
- 16 ounces cool whip

Direction

- Mix together cream cheese and sweetened condensed milk.
- Fold in whipped cream.
- Crush up cookies into smaller chunks, not so fine you do not get to bite into them.
- Add cookies to the whip cream mixture.
- Fold gently.
- Cool and eat.
- You can eat this as is in serving cups, or pour into a graham cracker crust. Whatever makes you happy!

149. Oreo Mousse Recipe

Serving: 24 | Prep: | Cook: | Ready in:

Ingredients

- 1 pkg. Oreos
- 1 stick butter-melted
- 2- 8oz. cream cheese
- 2 cups sugar
- 1 -16 oz. Cool Whip
- 1 large chocolate instant pudding

Direction

- Crush Oreos
- Save 3/4 cup for topping
- Mix melted butter and crushed cookies
- Put in 9 x 13 pan
- Mix cream cheese and sugar and 1/2 of Cool Whip
- Put on cookie crust.
- Mix pudding according to directions on box.
- Put on top of cream cheese mixture
- Top with Cool Whip and Cookies.

150. Party Size Chocolate Cherry Mousse Recipe

Serving: 20 | Prep: | Cook: 5mins | Ready in:

Ingredients

- 2 pkg, 12 0z each top quality semi sweet chocolate morsels
- 1 pkg, 6 0z top quality semi sweet chocolate morsels
- 3 cups heavy cream
- 1 lb jar of pitted sweet or sour cherries red or black - dained ,reserve cherry liquid
- 1 dozen eggs, room temperature separated, clean uncracked
- 1/4 cup sugar
- Garnish: whipped cream rosettes and maraschino cherries garnish if desired

Direction

- Prep time does not include chilling time
- Place chocolate in a heavy duty sauce pot with 12 Tbsp. of reserved cherry liquid and melt chocolate over lowest heat until melted in smooth.
- One can do this in a microwave bowl, microwaving high power for several minutes, checking to make sure mixture is melting and stirring till smooth.
- Either way, one must not overcook chocolate or it will seize and harden.
- When chocolate is stirred smooth, set aside to cool a bit

- Beat in yolks one at a time to incorporate well
- In another large bowel, whip cream to soft peaks and then gently fold into cooled chocolate.
- Stir in the drained cherries.
- With clean beaters beat whites till foamy and then increase speed and beat till almost stiff.
- Gradually add sugar and beat till stiff but not dry.
- Fold egg whites into chocolate mixture gently until well blended.
- Place mixture into a glass punch bowl if you have it, cover with plastic wrap and chill overnight.
- Then garnish as desired.
- Yield: 20 or more 1/2 cup servings
- Note: recipe may be reduced easily for smaller quantities
- Note: one may substitute a bit of Kirsch or cherry brandy for the cherry liquid if desired

151. Passion Fruit Mousse Recipe

Serving: 8 | Prep: | Cook: 10mins | Ready in:

Ingredients

- 2 cups frozen passion fruit pulp, defrosted
- 4 cups heavy cream
- 1 (14-ounce) can sweetened condensed milk
- mint sprigs, for garnish
- Biscotti or other crisp cookies, for garnish

Direction

- Special Equipment: martini glasses
- Place 1 tablespoon of passion fruit pulp in the bottom of 8 martini glasses or ramekins, totalling in 1/2 cup passion fruit pulp, set them aside.
- Using an electric mixer beat the cream until it holds stiff peaks. Whisk 1 1/4 cups of passion fruit pulp with the condensed milk in a large bowl, add 1/4 of the whipped cream and whisk it in.
- Fold in the remaining whipped cream and fill martini glasses or ramekins with some mousse.
- Drizzle some of the remaining passion fruit pulp over the top.
- Serve immediately or cover flush with plastic wrap and refrigerate for up to 8 hours.
- Serve cold with a mint sprig and a biscotti.

152. Passionfruit And White Chocolate Mousse Recipe

Serving: 4 | Prep: | Cook: 10mins | Ready in:

Ingredients

- 150g white chocolate
- 200ml fresh passionfruit pulp
- 3 eggs, separated
- 200ml thickened cream
- 1 ½ tbsp caster sugar
- whipped cream, to serve

Direction

- Place the chocolate and passion fruit in a heatproof bowl over a saucepan of simmering water (make sure bowl doesn't touch the water). Use a metal spoon to stir for 3-4 minutes or until the chocolate melts and the mixture is smooth. Set aside for 5 minutes to cool. Add the egg yolks and whisk until combined.
- Use an electric beater to beat the egg whites and sugar in a clean, dry bowl until firm peaks form. Fold the egg white mixture into the chocolate mixture until combined. Divide the mousse among three 200ml capacity serving dishes. Cover with plastic wrap and place in fridge for 4 hours until set.

153. Peach Mousse Recipe

Serving: 4 | Prep: | Cook: 5mins | Ready in:

Ingredients

- 1-1/2 cups diced peaches
- 2 tablespoons lemon juice
- 1/2 cup plain yogurt stirred
- 1/2 cup cottage cheese
- 1 packet unflavored gelatin
- 1/4 cup water
- 1/4 cup peach nectar
- 1 teaspoon ground ginger
- 1/4 cup sugar
- 1/2 cup whipped topping

Direction

- Puree peaches and lemon juice in a food processor.
- Mix together the yogurt and cottage cheese.
- Stir mixture by hand into the pureed fruit.
- Dissolve gelatine in the water in a small saucepan over low heat.
- Add nectar, ginger and sugar then cook for 2 minutes.
- Add peach mixture to the gelatine and mix well.
- Place mixture into a pint container and freeze until mixture looks thick about 30 minutes.
- Fold whipped topping into peach mixture and refrigerate for several hours.
- Spoon into individual dishes and serve.

154. Peanut Butter Mousse Cake Recipe

Serving: 12 | Prep: | Cook: 240mins | Ready in:

Ingredients

- Crust:
- 1 1/4 c. chocolate cooke crumbs (Oreo)
- 1/4 c finely chopped peanuts
- 3 T sugar
- 1/2 tsp. cinnamon
- 1/4 c. melted butter
- Mousse:
- 1 1/4 c. peanut butter
- 1-8 oz. pkg. cream cheese
- 1 1/4 c. icing sugar
- 1 T vanilla
- 1 1/3 c. whipping cream
- Topping:
- 1/3 c. whipping cream
- 3 T sugar
- 2 tsp. instant coffee powder
- 4 oz. semi sweet chopped chocolate
- 1/2 tsp. vanilla

Direction

- Crust:
- Heat oven 325. Stir together crumbs, peanuts, sugar & cinnamon. Add melted butter, stir until evenly moistened. Press into bottom and up sides of 9" springform pan. Bake 10 minutes, then cool.
- Mousse:
- Beat PB & cream cheese on low until blended. Add sugar and 1 T vanilla, beat until smooth. In large bowl, beat 1 1/3 c. whipping cream until soft peaks form, fold in PB mixture in 3 additions. Pour into crust. Place in fridge while preparing topping.
- Topping:
- Place cream, sugar, coffee powder in small saucepan. Heat until sugar dissolves and bubbles begin to form around edge. Remove from heat, add chocolate and stir until smooth. Add vanilla. Cool 5 minutes. Spread topping evenly over mouse filling. Cover & refrigerate until well chilled at least 4 hours.

155. Pear Mousse Recipe

Serving: 6 | Prep: | Cook: 20mins | Ready in:

Ingredients

- 3 very large ripe (for example Royal Riviera) pears or 6 smaller ones
- 1/2 cup butter melted
- 1 cup sugar
- 2 Tbs fresh lemon juice
- 1/4 cup brandy
- 1 cup heavy cream

Direction

- Peel and core pears and chop coarsely.
- Place pears in pot with sugar and butter and lemon juice and cook and stir over low heat 15 to 20 minutes.
- Let cool slightly and place in blender and puree smooth.
- Add the brandy and mix well.
- Cool completely.
- Whip heavy cream and blend into cooled pear mixture.
- Chill well for several hours.
- Serve in dessert glasses and garnish with a mint sprig.
- Or serve to garnish chocolate cake

156. Pears With Chocolate Mousse And White Sauce Recipe

Serving: 4 | Prep: | Cook: 30mins | Ready in:

Ingredients

- for 4 persons:
- 4 pears (well shaped)
- for the syrup:
- 1 kg sugar
- 2 kg water
- for the filling (chocolate mousse):
- 150 g bitter chocolate
- 60 g milk
- 40 g syrup
- 360 g freash cream (35% fat)
- for the sauce:
- 60 g white chocolate
- 30 g milk
- 70 g fresh cream (35% fat)
- fresh mint
- 1 fresh vanilla stick

Direction

- Pierce a hole in the center of each pear and remove the interior. Peel afterwards. Make sure not to remove the stems. Pour lemon juice to preserve the colour of the pears. Place the fruits in a casserole. Add the sugar, water and a lemon zest. Simmer for 20 minutes with the lid semi open. Take care to preserve the shape of the pears. Do not boil too much.
- Whip the fresh cream in a bowl with a mixer.
- Bring the milk and the syrup to a boil and mix them with the bitter chocolate in a large bowl, stirring until the chocolate melts.
- When the temperature drops, use a spatula to mix the melted chocolate with the fresh cream and place the mousse in the fridge. Use a saucepan to prepare the sauce.
- Mix the milk with the fresh cream and one vanilla stick.
- Stir until the mixture becomes warm, then add the white chocolate and stir again, until the mixture becomes smooth.
- Finish off with a touch of mint.
- Fill the pears with the mousse and serve with the white chocolate sauce. Perfect!

157. Pecan And Chocolate Mousse Twinkie Dessert Recipe

Serving: 16 | Prep: | Cook: 120mins | Ready in:

Ingredients

- 9 Twinkies
- 3 eggs; separated
- 1/2 c. sugar
- 1/2 t .vanilla

- 6 oz. semisweet chocolate chips
- 1 c .pecans; chopped
- 1 c. heavy cream; whipped
- 1/8 t. cream of tartar

Direction

- Grease casserole dish with butter or non-stick spray.
- Cut 8 Twinkies in thirds, lengthwise, and put one layer on the bottom of the casserole.
- Beat egg whites, with the cream of tartar and sugar, adding vanilla. Melt chocolate chips in the top of a double boiler.
- Add egg yolks to chocolate, 1 at a time, continuing to stir over boiling water. (Let chocolate cool to lukewarm so that it will not melt the egg whites.)
- Fold chocolate into egg whites.
- Spread chocolate mousse over Twinkies, then sprinkle with about half of the nuts.
- Layer on more Twinkies, more chocolate, more nuts. Continue layering.
- Top with whipped cream and garnish with chopped pecans and chocolate shavings if desired.
- Chill and serve.

158. Pineapple Mousse Recipe

Serving: 8 | Prep: | Cook: | Ready in:

Ingredients

- pineapple Mousse
- Preparation time: 25 minutes
- Chilling time: 3 hours
- --
- Cut lengthwise:
- 1 ripe pineapple
- Scoop out fruit from both halves, removing the core.
- Finely chop the fruit, reserving juice.
- Mix pineapple with:
- 1 1/2 tablespoons lime juice
- 1/2 cup honey
- 2 cups heavy cream, whipped

Direction

- Spoon mixture into an 8-inch square pan.
- Place in freezer for approximately 3 hours or until slightly firm.
- (To make this dish ahead of time, freeze the pineapple mixture solid and then remove from freezer 20 minutes before serving to allow it to soften.)
- Serve garnished with:
- Slices of kiwi and sprigs of fresh mint
- Note: A suggestion on the pineapple.
- This sounds great. I learned from experience that if you wait to cut the pineapple until 2 or 3 rows of leaves are dried at the base, it will be as sweet as candy when you cut it open. Mmmm!

159. Prune Mousse Recipe

Serving: 8 | Prep: | Cook: 60mins | Ready in:

Ingredients

- 1 package (9oz) pitted prunes
- 1/4 tsp salt
- 8 oz sour cream
- 1 qt. milk
- 1 qt half and half
- 4 heaping Tablespoons flour
- 1 cup sugar
- 3 teaspoons cinnamon

Direction

- Stew the prunes in enough water to cover them until they are very soft and starting to fall apart.
- Drain and allow to cool.
- In a large saucepan and over low heat, whisk the flour with a little milk at a time to wet it and keep it from lumping. Once it is

incorporated into enough milk, add the remaining milk, salt, sour cream, and half and half. Heat slowly to just below scalding or until the mixture thickens, whisking constantly. Remove from heat and cool. While cooling, mix the sugar and cinnamon together in a small bowl and slowly whisk it into the cooled thickened gravy. Then add the drained stewed prunes and mix well. Refrigerate and let age at least 24 hours before serving.
- I also have a gluten free version I developed for my mother who has celiac sprue if anyone is interested.

160. Pumpkin Mousse

Serving: 6 | Prep: | Cook: 360mins | Ready in:

Ingredients

- 1 package (8 ounces) cream cheese, softened
- 1/4 cup sugar
- 1 can (15 ounces) solid-pack pumpkin
- 1 package (3.4 ounces) instant vanilla pudding mix
- 2 teaspoons pumpkin pie spice
- 1 cup cold 2% milk
- 1-3/4 cups whipped topping
- 24 gingersnaps, divided

Direction

- In a large bowl, beat cream cheese and sugar until smooth; add pumpkin, pudding mix and pie spice. Gradually beat in milk. Fold in whipped topping.
- Spoon 1/4 cup mousse into eight serving dishes. Crumble 16 gingersnaps; sprinkle over mousse. Top each with remaining mousse. Refrigerate until serving. Top with whole gingersnap just before serving.

161. Pumpkin Mousse Parfait Recipe

Serving: 9 | Prep: | Cook: 30mins | Ready in:

Ingredients

- 1/4 cup dark rum
- 1 packet (2 teaspoons) unflavored gelatin powder
- 1 (15-ounce can) pumpkin (not pie filling)
- 1/2 cup granulated sugar
- 1/2 cup light brown sugar, lightly packed
- 2 extra-large egg yolks
- 2 teaspoons grated orange zest
- 1/2 teaspoon ground cinnamon
- 1/4 teaspoon ground nutmeg
- 1/2 teaspoon kosher salt
- 1 1/2 cups cold heavy cream
- 1 1/2 teaspoons pure vanilla extract
- sweetened whipped cream
- 8 to 10 chopped ginger cookies
- crystallized ginger, for decoration, optional

Direction

- Place the rum in a heat-proof bowl and sprinkle the gelatine over it. Set aside for 10 minutes for the gelatine to soften.
- In a large bowl, whisk together the pumpkin, granulated sugar, brown sugar, egg yolks, orange zest, cinnamon, nutmeg, and salt. Set the bowl of gelatine over a pan of simmering water and cook until the gelatine is clear.
- Immediately whisk the hot gelatine mixture into the pumpkin mixture. In the bowl of an electric mixer fitted with a whisk attachment, whip the heavy cream and vanilla until soft peaks form.
- Fold the whipped cream into the pumpkin mixture.
- To assemble, spoon some of the pumpkin mixture into parfait glasses, add a layer of whipped cream, then some chopped cookies.
- Repeat, ending with a third layer of pumpkin.
- Cover with plastic wrap and refrigerate for 4 hours or overnight.

- To serve, decorate with whipped cream and slivered crystallized ginger

162. Pumpkin Mousse Recipe

Serving: 6 | Prep: | Cook: 10mins | Ready in:

Ingredients

- 1 carton (4 oz) whipped cream cheese with cinnamon and brown sugar
- 1 c pumpkin pie filling
- 1/2 c whipped topping
- 6 individual graham cracker tart shells
- Additional whipped topping and cinnamon

Direction

- In small bowl, combine cream cheese and pumpkin till blended. Fold in whipped topping. Fill tart shells. Garnish each with additional whipped topping and sprinkle with cinnamon. Store in refrigerator.
- If you can't find cream cheese with cinnamon and brown sugar, you can add your own to taste.

163. Pumpkin Mousse In Cinnamon Pastry Shells Recipe

Serving: 8 | Prep: | Cook: 10mins | Ready in:

Ingredients

- 2 boxes (10 oz. each) frozen puff pastry shells
- 3 tablespoons melted butter
- cinnamon sugar *
- 1 can (30 oz.) LIBBY'S® Easy pumpkin Pie Mix
- 1 box (3.4 oz.) vanilla instant pudding and pie filling mix
- 2 teaspoons ground cinnamon
- 1 cup frozen whipped topping, thawed

Direction

- PREHEAT oven to 400° F.
- PLACE pastry shells on baking sheet.
- Brush tops with butter and sprinkle with cinnamon-sugar.
- Bake according to package directions.
- Cool to room temperature.
- Remove tops and reserve for garnish.
- Remove soft pastry inside shells and discard.
- BEAT pumpkin pie mix, pudding mix and cinnamon in large mixer bowl on medium speed for 2 minutes.
- Gently fold in whipped topping.
- Spoon about 1/3 cup pumpkin mousse into each pastry shell.
- Top with pastry tops.
- Serve immediately.
- For cinnamon sugar:
- Combine 1 tablespoon granulated sugar and 1/2 teaspoon ground cinnamon in small bowl.

164. Pumpkin Pudding Whip Recipe

Serving: 0 | Prep: | Cook: 15mins | Ready in:

Ingredients

- 2 c. canned pumpkin
- 1 pkg. sugar-free instant butterscotch pudding
- 1 pkg. sugar-free instant vanilla pudding
- 1 12-oz can evaporated milk
- 1 cup coconut and/or 1/2 pkg mini chocolate chips or sugar free chocolate chips (optional)
- cinnamon

Direction

- Combine pumpkin, puddings and milks in a bowl and beat until smooth and thick. Fold in coconut and/or chocolate chips, if desired. Spoon into individual dishes and top with a sprinkling of cinnamon.

165. Quick And Easy Chocolate Mousse Recipe

Serving: 4 | Prep: | Cook: 3mins | Ready in:

Ingredients

- * 6 ounce package of semi-sweet chocolate morsels
- * 3 eggs, separated
- * 1/4 cup water
- * 1/8 tsp salt
- * 1/3 cup firmly packed brown sugar

Direction

- # Melt the semi-sweet chocolate morsels over hot (not boiling) water.
- # Remove from heat.
- # Add the egg yolks, one at a time.
- # Beat well after each addition.
- # Add water and beat until smooth.
- # In a bowl, combine egg whites and salt.
- # Beat until soft peaks form.
- # Gradually beat in brown sugar and continue beating until stiff peaks form.
- # Gently fold in chocolate mixture.
- # Chill in the refrigerator a couple of hours or until ready to serve.

166. Quick Mousse L'orange Recipe

Serving: 0 | Prep: | Cook: 30mins | Ready in:

Ingredients

- Quick Mousse L'orange
- 2/3 cup hot water
- 2 envelopes unflavored gelatin
- 1/3 cup sugar
- 6 oz can orange juice concentrate
- 2 tablespoon unflavored yogurt
- 1 teaspoon orange extract
- 2 cup ice cubes
- There is several ways you can make this, one option would be to use heavy whipping cream and it would make the process faster. A even faster and cheaper way that I have used when in a bind is to use Cool Whip and some orange kool-aid, not the best, but it worked.

Direction

- In blender, mix together hot water and gelatine. Add sugar and blend. Add orange juice, yogurt, extract, and ice and blend on high until ice is crushed. Pour into parfait glasses and chill. Dessert will be ready to eat in 10 minutes. You could also serve in small pastry cups.

167. Quick And Easy Chocolate Mousse Recipe

Serving: 4 | Prep: | Cook: 120mins | Ready in:

Ingredients

- 6 ounce package of semi-sweet chocolate morsels
- 3 eggs, separated
- 1/4 cup water
- 1/8 tsp salt
- 1/3 cup firmly packed brown sugar

Direction

- Melt the semi-sweet chocolate morsels over hot (not boiling) water.
- Remove from heat.
- Add the egg yolks, one at a time.
- Beat well after each addition.
- Add water and beat until smooth.
- In a bowl, combine egg whites and salt.
- Beat until soft peaks form.
- Gradually beat in brown sugar and continue beating until stiff peaks form.

168. Raspberry And Chocolate Yogurt Desert Recipe

Serving: 2 | Prep: | Cook: 20mins | Ready in:

Ingredients

- Plain probiotic yogurt
- 10 squares of bittersweet chocolate
- 15 raspberries
- 1 tbsp of sugar
- 1 tsp of chilli powder
- 1 tbsp of vanilla extract
- 5 tablespoons of water.
- Rasberries and almond for sprinkling.

Direction

- Melt chocolate
- Combine melted chocolate with yogurt, vanilla and chilli.
- Spoon into moulds and freeze overnight
- Put raspberries, sugar and water into blender and blend.
- Strain raspberry sauce into pot and simmer for 3 minutes before serving.
- To serve turn yogurt mix out of moulds onto plates. Spoon some flaked almonds and fresh raspberries over them and pour the sauce on them.

169. Raspberry Mousse Recipe

Serving: 8 | Prep: | Cook: 20mins | Ready in:

Ingredients

- Raspberry Mousse
- 3 c raspberries, fresh OR
- 30 oz raspberries, frozen,
- -- thawed, and drained
- -- (liquid reserved)
- 1/2 c sugar
- 3 T water, cold
- 1 T syrup, corn, light
- 3 egg whites
- 1/2 lemon, juice of
- 2 c Cream, whipping

Direction

- For Mousse:
- Choose a few perfect raspberries for garnish and set aside. Puree remaining raspberries in processor or blender until very smooth. Transfer 2 tablespoons of puree, with seeds, to measuring cup. Strain remaining puree into mixing bowl, eliminating all seeds. Add enough strained puree to the 2 tablespoons to measure 1/2 cup. Set aside. Chill remaining strained puree, which will be used as sauce.
- In a small heavy saucepan combine sugar, water, and corn syrup. Bring slowly to boil over medium heat, stirring occasionally and brushing down any sugar crystals from sides of pan with brush dipped in cold water. Raise heat slightly and cook until temperature of syrup reaches 240 F (soft ball stage).
- While syrup is cooking, beat 3 egg whites in a mixer until stiff. As soon as syrup reaches 240 F, lower mixer speed to slow and pour hot syrup onto beaten whites, in a very thing stream. When all of the syrup has been incorporated, raise a mixer speed and beat meringue until cool.
- Stir together the 1/2 cup reserved raspberry puree and lemon juice and fold into the meringue until nearly blended. Whip cream until stiff and fold into the meringue until blended. DO NOT OVERMIX.

170. Raspberry White Chocolate Mousse Recipe

Serving: 8 | Prep: | Cook: 10mins | Ready in:

Ingredients

- 1 package sweetened frozen raspberries thawed
- 2 tablespoons granulated sugar
- 1 tablespoon orange juice concentrate
- 2 cups heavy whipping cream
- 6 ounces white baking chocolate
- 1 teaspoon vanilla extract
- 1/4 cup milk chocolate chips
- 1 teaspoon vanilla

Direction

- Combine raspberries, sugar and orange juice in blender and process until smooth.
- Press through a sieve then discard seeds and refrigerate sauce.
- In sauce pan over low heat cook and stir cream and white chocolate until chocolate is melted.
- Transfer to mixing bowl then cover and refrigerate 6 hours stirring occasionally.
- Beat cream mixture on high speed until light and fluffy but do not over beat.
- Just before serving melt chocolate chips and oil in microwave.
- Spoon 2 tablespoons raspberry sauce on each plate.
- Spoon 1/2 cup chocolate mousse over sauce then drizzle with melted chocolate.

171. Red Raspberry Mousse Recipe

Serving: 4 | Prep: | Cook: | Ready in:

Ingredients

- 1 pint fresh raspberries
- 1 tablespoon fresh lemon juice
- 1 cup heavy cream
- 1 egg white
- 1/4 cup sugar

Direction

- Place raspberries in blender container and blend until smooth.
- Add lemon juice.
- In large bowl beat cream until soft peaks from then fold in raspberry mixture.
- Sprinkle sugar over egg white and continue beating until sugar is dissolved then fold into raspberry mixture.
- Spoon into parfait glasses then cover and freeze.
- Remove from freezer 15 minutes before serving.

172. Rich Chocolate Mousse Recipe

Serving: 4 | Prep: | Cook: | Ready in:

Ingredients

- 150g dark chocolate
- 1 C evaporated milk thoroughly chilled
- 2 Tbsp Castor sugar
- 1 Tbsp Gelatiine
- 2 Tbsp hot water
- 2 eggs seperated

Direction

- In a microwave jug combine chocolate and 1/4 of the milk.
- Heat on 100% power for 30 seconds then reduce power to 30% and continue cooking, stirring every minute, until all is melted and smooth.
- Dissolve gelatine in hot water and add to chocolate mixture.
- Mix in egg yolks and stir well.

- Whip rest of evaporated milk and egg whites until thick then slowly add chocolate mix.
- Pour into 4 serving dishes, decorate if desired and refrigerate for 2 hours.

173. Ricotta Mousse With Berries Recipe

Serving: 4 | Prep: | Cook: 15mins | Ready in:

Ingredients

- 1 c lt. ricotta cheese
- 2 Tbs orange liqueur
- 1/2 tsp finely shredded orange peel
- 1/2 c fresh, sliced strawberries
- 1/2 c fresh raspberries
- 1/2 c fresh blueberries
- 1/2 c fresh blackberries
- 1 tsp lemon juice
- 1/2 to 1 tsp Splenda or 2 tsp honey
- fresh mint leaves (optional)

Direction

- In small bowl, whisk together ricotta, 1 Tbsp. orange liqueur and orange peel. Cover and chill 1 hour to overnight.
- In med. bowl, combine the berries, lemon juice and remaining 1 Tbsp. liqueur. Cover and let stand at room temperature 15 mins to develop flavours.
- To serve, divide fruit mixture among 4 dessert dishes, spooning any juices atop fruit in dishes. Top with ricotta mixture. Sprinkle individual servings with Splenda or drizzle with honey. If desired, garnish with mint.

174. Simple Chocolate Mousse Recipe

Serving: 6 | Prep: | Cook: 15mins | Ready in:

Ingredients

- 1-1/2 c semi-sweet chocolate chips (8oz)
- salt
- 1-1/2 c heavy whipping cream
- 1-1/2 Tbs confectioners sugar (or to taste)

Direction

- Chill a large bowl with a whisk in freezer for about 10 mins.
- In top of double boiler over simmering water, stir the chocolate chips until just melted, about 4 mins.
- Add a pinch of salt. Meanwhile, whip the heavy cream and confectioners' sugar till the cream holds its shape. Remove the chocolate from the heat and using a rubber spatula, fold half of the cream into the chocolate, incorporating it completely.
- Quickly fold the remaining cream into the chocolate. Spoon the mousse into serving dishes and serve at once.

175. Simple Strawberry Mousse Recipe

Serving: 34 | Prep: | Cook: 3mins | Ready in:

Ingredients

- 2c. frozen strawberries
- 1pkg.(8oz) low fat cream cheese, cut into small cubes.
- 1/2c. confectioners sugar (powdered sugar)
- 1 container whipped topping, 4 oz thawed.

Direction

- 1.) In a blender or food processor w/ chopping blade, combine strawberries, cream cheese, and sugar. Cover and process until mixture is smooth, scraping side as necessary.
- 2.) Pour mixture into a mixing bowl. Fold in whipped topping
- 3.) Spoon mousse mixture into desert dishes.

- 4.) Chill for 3 hours or overnight* overnight is better it marinades in the flavours will marry and get all nice and excited. lol!
- Serve and enjoy

176. Simply Chocolate Mousse Recipe

Serving: 7 | Prep: | Cook: 10mins | Ready in:

Ingredients

- 1 cup semisweet chocolate chips
- 5 tablespoons boiling water
- 4 eggs, separated
- Garnish: whipped cream

Direction

- Grind chocolate chips in a blender, using short pulses.
- Add boiling water and blend to melt the chocolate.
- Add egg yolks, one at a time, blending well after each.
- In a medium bowl, beat egg whites with electric mixer until stiff peaks form.
- Fold egg whites into chocolate mixture gently.
- Pour the mousse into serving glasses and chill in refrigerator until set. Makes about 7 servings

177. Slow Cooker Chocolate Mocha Mousse Recipe

Serving: 6 | Prep: | Cook: 120mins | Ready in:

Ingredients

- 2 cups heavy cream
- 4 large egg yolks
- 3 tablespoons sugar
- 1 teaspoon vanilla extract
- 1/3 cup cold, strong coffee
- 2 cups semisweet chocolate chips
- To serve: whipped cream or berries (optional)

Direction

- Use a 4-quart slow cooker.
- Put the heavy cream, egg yolks, sugar, vanilla and coffee into your crock.
- Mix until combined with a whisk.
- You don't need to go crazy, just mix well.
- Add the chocolate chips.
- Cover and cook on HIGH for about 1 hour or on LOW for about 2 hours.
- You are looking for little bubbles in the surface of the cream and melted chocolate.
- VERY VERY VERY carefully, pour the mixture in to a blender. You'll get about 2 1/2 to 3 cups of liquid.
- Blend on HIGH, until it 'grows' to about 5 to 6 cups and doesn't seem it will rise any higher.
- Pour into serving dishes; I used wine glasses.
- Chill for 2 hours in the refrigerator.
- Cover with plastic wrap to prevent skin formation on top
- Top with whipped cream or berries or nothing at all.

178. Square Deals Recipe

Serving: 12 | Prep: | Cook: 1hours | Ready in:

Ingredients

- [section]Crust[\section]
- 1 package chocolate graham crackers (finely crushed)
- 1/2 cup salted butter, melted
- 1 Tablespoon brown sugar
- 1/4 cup toffee bits (crushed)
- [section]Filling[\section]
- 1 cup heavy whipping cream, whipped until stiff peaks form (set aside)

- 1 package (8 oz) cream cheese, softened
- 1 cup creamy peanut butter
- 2 teaspoons clear vanilla extract
- 1/2 teaspoon cinnamon
- 1/4 teaspoon salt
- 1/2 cup toffee bits (broken)
- [section]Topping[\section]
- 6 oz semi-chocolate chips
- 1/2 cup heavy whipping cream
- 1/4 cup chopped salted peanuts
- 1/4 cup creamy peanut butter
- 1/4 cup mini chocolate chips

Direction

- Preheat oven to 350 degrees.
- Using square brownie muffin pans, line with foil/paper muffin liners and use fingers to fit as squares.
- In food processor, mix together crust ingredients. Spoon evenly into square muffin pan, using fingers (or spoon) to pat down. Bake for 7 minutes. Let cool.
- Using stand mixer and beater whip heavy whipping cream until stiff peaks form and set aside. Using flat blade, add all remaining filling ingredients (except whipped cream). Remove from stand and fold in the whipped cream until mixed. Spoon filling into each square muffin pan and place in freezer for 1 hour.
- Melt chocolate chips and 1/2 cup heavy whipping cream in microwave in 30 second intervals (stirring after each 30 seconds) until melted and mixed. Spoon chocolate mixture onto each square muffin. Using cake frosting with small hole tip, pipe creamy peanut butter in zigzag pattern on each muffin square. Sprinkle chopped peanuts and mini chocolate chips.
- Remove muffin liners just before serving.

179. Strawberry Jello Mousse Recipe

Serving: 6 | Prep: | Cook: | Ready in:

Ingredients

- 1 package (4 serving size) strawberry jello
- ¾ cup boiling water
- 2 cups thawed Cool Whip Topping
- 1 cup ice cubes or crushed ice
- 1 ½ cups strawberries, chopped finely or mashed

Direction

- Combine the jello with the boiling water until it has dissolved, then add the ice and stir well.
- Add the strawberries and half of the whipped topping and stir again.
- Spoon this mixture into 6 serving glasses and refrigerate them for a couple of hours until firm.
- Top with the remaining cool whip and serve chilled.

180. Strawberry Margarita Mousse Recipe

Serving: 6 | Prep: | Cook: 10mins | Ready in:

Ingredients

- 4 eggs, separated
- 3/4 cup sugar
- 1 (3-ounce) box strawberry flavored gelatin
- 1/4 teaspoon salt
- 1/4 cup fresh lemon juice
- 1/4 cup fresh lime juice
- 1/4 cup limeade
- 1/4 cup fresh orange juice
- 3 tablespoons red food coloring
- 1 teaspoon grated lime zest
- 3/4 teaspoon cream of tartar
- 1 cup heavy cream, whipped until stiff

- 1 cup small diced strawberries
- Red sanding sugar, for garnish
- Strawberry slices and fresh mint, for garnish

Direction

- Beat the egg yolks in a bowl until light.
- In a medium saucepan, stir together 1/4 cup of the sugar, gelatine and salt.
- Stir in the beaten egg yolks, lemon juice, lime juice, limeade, orange juice, and turn the heat onto medium.
- Gently stir the mixture over the heat until the sugar, salt and gelatine have dissolved completely.
- Remove from heat and transfer to a large mixing bowl.
- Cool to room temperature, stir in the food colouring and lime zest and then place in the refrigerator to chill.
- Stir the mixture occasionally until it begins to set, about 30 minutes.
- Meanwhile, with an electric mixer, beat the egg whites and cream of tartar until foamy.
- Gradually add the remaining 1/2 cup sugar to the whites, beating constantly, until stiff and glossy.
- Remove the gelled mixture from the refrigerator and fold in the diced strawberries.
- Next, add the meringue and whipped cream and thoroughly fold everything together.
- Chill in the refrigerator for 1 hour.
- Pour the red sanding sugar out into a shallow bowl or pie plate, at least 1/4-inch high.
- Dampen a thick paper towel, folded in quarters, with water.
- Press the rims of 6 (8-ounce) margarita glasses onto the wet paper towel and then lightly dip them into the sanding sugar.
- Divide the mousse into the margarita glasses with a spoon. Garnish the tops of each mousse glass with freshly sliced strawberries and mint leaves.

181. Strawberry Mousse Parfait Recipe

Serving: 4 | Prep: | Cook: 1mins | Ready in:

Ingredients

- 1 1/3 cups quartered strawberries (from 6 oz)
- 1 tablespoon sugar
- 1 teaspoon fresh lemon juice
- 3/4 teaspoon unflavored gelatin (from 1 envelope)
- 1 1/2 tablespoons water
- 1/3 cup well-chilled heavy cream
- 3 butter cookies, coarsely crushed (1/4 cup)

Direction

- Preparation: Mash 1 cup quartered strawberries with sugar and lemon juice in a bowl using a fork. Cut remaining strawberries into 1/4-inch dice and reserve.
- Sprinkle gelatine evenly over water in a very small saucepan and let stand 1 minute to soften, then warm over low heat, stirring until gelatine is dissolved. Stir gelatine mixture into mashed strawberries.
- Set bowl in a larger bowl of ice and cold water and stir frequently until a spoonful of gelatine mixture holds its shape briefly before dissolving back into mixture, about 5 minutes.
- Beat cream in another bowl with a whisk until it just holds stiff peaks. Fold 1/2 cup whipped cream into gelatine mixture, then fold in 1/4 cup diced strawberries (reserve remainder for topping).
- Spoon one third of strawberry mousse into a glass and sprinkle evenly with half of cookie crumbs, then top with half of remaining mousse and all of remaining cookie crumbs. Top with remaining mousse, whipped cream, and strawberries, then chill until set, about 30 minutes.

182. Strawberry Mousse Recipe

Serving: 6 | Prep: | Cook: | Ready in:

Ingredients

- 1 quart strawberries
- 1/2 cup granulated sugar
- 3 envelopes unflavored gelatin
- 1/2 cup cold water
- 1 cup boiling water
- 2 cups whipping cream
- 1/2 cup sifted powdered sugar
- Whole and sliced strawberries

Direction

- Puree 1 quart of strawberries in container of blender.
- Add 1/2 cup sugar and process until blended.
- Soften gelatine in 1/2 cup cold water in a large bowl.
- Add boiling water stirring until gelatine completely dissolves then cool.
- Stir strawberry mixture into gelatine then chill until consistency of unbeaten egg white.
- Beat cream until foamy then gradually add powdered sugar and beat until soft peaks form.
- Fold whipped cream into strawberry mixture then spoon into lightly oiled mould.
- Refrigerate until set then remove to serving plate and garnish with strawberries.

183. Strawberry Mousse Squares Recipe

Serving: 1 | Prep: | Cook: | Ready in:

Ingredients

- 2/3 cup boiling water
- 1 pkg. (4-serving size)Strawberry Flavor gelatin
- 18 OREO chocolate Sandwich cookies, crushed
- 1/4 cup (1/2 stick) butter, melted
- 1 pkg. (8 oz.) cream cheese, softened
- 2-1/2 cups thawed Cool Whip whipped topping, divided
- 3 cups small strawberries, sliced, divided

Direction

- Stir boiling water into dry gelatine mix in small bowl at least 2 min. until completely dissolved. Cool 5 min., stirring occasionally.
- Meanwhile, mix cookie crumbs and butter; press onto bottom of 13x9-inch pan.
- Beat cream cheese in large bowl with electric mixer on medium speed until creamy. Gradually add gelatine, beating well after each addition. Gently stir in 1-1/2 cups each of the whipped topping and strawberries. Spoon over crust.
- Refrigerate 1 hour or until firm. Cover with remaining whipped topping. Serve topped with the remaining strawberries. Store leftovers in refrigerator.

184. Strawberry Mousse Torte Recipe

Serving: 8 | Prep: | Cook: | Ready in:

Ingredients

- 2 (.25 ounce) envelopes KNOX unflavored gelatin
- 1/2 cup cold water
- 1 pint strawberries, divided
- 3/4 cup sugar
- 3/4 cup milk
- 2 cups Cool Whip whipped topping, divided
- 39 NILLA chocolate wafers, divided

Direction

- Sprinkle gelatine over cold water in small saucepan; let stand 1 minute. Cook over low heat 2 minutes or until gelatine is completely dissolved.

- Halve 4 of the strawberries; reserve for garnish. Place remaining strawberries, sugar and milk in blender or food processor container; cover. Blend until smooth. Gradually add gelatine mixture through feed cap while processing until blended. Pour into medium bowl. Gently stir in 1 cup of the whipped topping with wire whisk; cover. Refrigerate 30 minutes or until slightly thickened.
- Line bottom and side of 9-inch springform pan with 35 wafers. Spoon thickened strawberry mixture into lined pan; cover. Refrigerate 2 hours or until firm.
- Crush remaining wafers. Top torte with remaining 1 cup whipped topping, wafer crumbs and halved strawberries.

185. Super Duper Easy Chocolate Mousse Recipe

Serving: 18 | Prep: | Cook: 20mins | Ready in:

Ingredients

- 2 cups 2% milk
- 3 eggs
- 6 tblsp sugar
- 24 oz bag of semi-sweet chocolate chips
- 4-6 tblsp liquor (I've used raspberry flavored, strawberry flavored, orange flavored, hazelnut flavored, coffee flavored, and Amaretto, but it can be any flavor that goes well with chocolate, such as banana, cherry or mint)

Direction

- In a sauce pan, boil the milk.
- Combine all other ingredients in a blender and puree as much as possible.
- Pour boiling milk into the blender, and liquefy. (The boiling milk cooks the eggs)
- Pour mousse either into a large bowl or individual serving dishes and chill overnight.

186. Swiss Chocolate Mousse Torte Recipe

Serving: 10 | Prep: | Cook: 15mins | Ready in:

Ingredients

- Swiss chocolate Mousse Torte
- COOKING TIME
- Active Time: 15 minutes
- Total Time: 8 hours and 15 minutes
- INGREDIENTS
- 12 chocolate Swiss roll cakes
- 1 brick (8 oz) cream cheese, softened
- 2 boxes (2.8 oz each) European Style milk chocolate Mousse Mix

Direction

- PREPARATION
- 1. Lightly coat an 8 x 3-in. springform pan with non-stick spray. Slice each cake into seven 1/4-in.-thick rounds. Arrange 2 rows around side of pan. Fit remaining slices to cover bottom of pan.
- 2. Beat cream cheese and 1/4 cup sugar in a large bowl with mixer on medium speed until smooth and fluffy. Prepare both boxes of mousse mix as label directs, using only 1 cup cold water total instead of the milk.
- 3. Fold 1/4 the mousse into the cream cheese mixture until no white streaks remain. Fold in remaining mousse until blended. Spoon into lined pan. Cover and refrigerate 8 hours, or overnight. To serve, remove pan sides.
- Different Takes
- Add 1/4 tsp. mint extract to the mousse.
- Nestlé mousse mix also comes in Milk Chocolate Irish Crème, Dark Chocolate and Mocha, any of which could be substituted.
- Garnish with dollops of whipped cream or additional slices of cake.

187. Szechuan Pepper Chocolate Mousse Recipe

Serving: 8 | Prep: | Cook: 10mins | Ready in:

Ingredients

- 1-1/4 Pounds bittersweet chocolate,chopped
- 2-1/2 Cups~plus~1/3 Cup heavy cream
- 4 Large Fresh egg yolks
- 3 Tablespoons water
- 2 Tablespoons honey
- 16 szechuan peppercorns,crushed

Direction

- Melt the chocolate in a saucepan over simmering water, stirring.
- Let cool for about 5 minutes.
- In bowl, beat 2-1/2 cups of the cream until soft peaks form.
- Working quickly, fold in the cooled chocolate.
- In a stainless steel bowl set over a pan of simmering water, whisk the egg yolks with the water, honey, and peppercorns, until double in volume, about 5 minutes.
- Remove the bowl from heat and with mixer, beat the sabayon on high until completely cool, about 5 minutes.
- Beat the remaining 1/3 cup of cream to soft peak stage, the fold into the sabayon.
- Using 2 Tablespoons, shape the chocolate mousse into a large egg like shape, and place on each china plate.
- Spoon the sabayon around the mousse and serve.
- Nice with Thin Butter Cookies

188. Tequila Mousse With Raspberry Sauce Recipe

Serving: 10 | Prep: | Cook: 10mins | Ready in:

Ingredients

- For the Soufle base
- 150 gr of egg whites
- 100 gr of egg yolks
- 100 gr of suggar
- 60 gr of cornstarch
- For the Mousse
- 60 gr of egg whithes
- 110 gr of suggar
- 250 gr of cream
- 40 gr of colapis
- 125 ml of tequila (the golden one prefered and you can add more if you want to)

Direction

- For the soufflé
- 1 Cream the egg yolks with half the sugar until they get almost white
- 2 Cream the egg whites with the other half sugar until you get medium peaks
- 3 Mix the yolks and the whites by hand with a whisk
- 4 Add the cornstarch and make sure you mix it right so you don't leave little balls on it.
- 5 Spread the mixture on an oven tin and take to the oven for about 15 -20 minutes at 300F
- For the mousse
- 1 place on a pot the egg whites and the sugar, take them to the heat until they get warm, but never stop beating, it will take 10 secs.
- 2 beat the whites until you get firm peaks
- 3 On warm water add the colapis and mix until you can´t see any lump
- 4 Add the colapis to the egg whites.
- 5 Whip the cream half the way
- 6 Mix the cream whit the egg whites by hand
- 7 add the tequila to the previous mixture
- 8 On a ring place a base of the cold soufflé and pour the mousse mixture.

- 9 Take to the refrigerator for about 2 or 3 hours.
- When it´s firm, I like to cover it with raspberry sauce (raspberry cooked with sugar at your taste and the drained)

189. Three Chocolate Mousse Cake Recipe

Serving: 12 | Prep: | Cook: 35mins | Ready in:

Ingredients

- Dark-chocolate layer:
- 8 oz. dark, or bitter-sweet chocolate chips
- 1/4 cup butter
- 2 tbsp. almond-flavored liqueur, or 1 tsp. almond extract
- 1/2 cup heavy cream, whipped to stiff peaks
- White-chocolate layer:
- 3/4 cup heavy cream
- 1 1/2 tsp. unflavored gelatin
- 6 oz. white chocolate chips
- 1/2 cup finely chopped almonds (can sub with walnuts)
- 1/2 cup heavy cream, whipped to stiff peaks
- Milk-chocolate layer:
- 8 0z. milk chocolate chips
- 1/4 cup butter
- 1 cup frozen raspberries, thawed, pureed and sieved to remove seeds
- 1/2 cup heavy cream, whipped to stiff peaks
- Raspberry sauce:
- 1 cup frozen raspberries, thawed
- 1 tbsp. cornstarch
- 1 tbsp. sugar
- unsweetened cocoa powder for decoration (optional)

Direction

- Grease an 8-inch loaf pan with non-stick cooking spray; line it with plastic wrap. Fill small roasting pan (or cookie pan) with dried beans. Wedge loaf pan into beans, tilting it lengthwise so that the first layer of dark chocolate mousse will be on one side of the pan. Note* instead of dried beans, I just use 2 small plates for support - one in the front and one in the back of the loaf pan. You just need something to keep it tilted until the mousse is hardened.
- Dark-chocolate layer: in saucepan over very low heat melt dark chocolate with butter, stirring constantly until smooth. Stir in liqueur or almond flavoring. Cool slightly. With a spatula, gently fold in the whipped cream. Pour mousse into loaf pan, smooth top. Refrigerate, tilted, until mousse is firm, about 1 hour.
- White-chocolate layer: In saucepan, combine 3/4 cup heavy cream and gelatine; let stand 5 minutes. Add white chocolate, heat over very low heat until melted, stirring constantly. Place pan in a bowl of ice water. Stir with a whisk until slightly thickened, for about 2 minutes. Remove from ice water, stir in almonds. With a spatula, gently fold in the whipped cream.
- Reposition the loaf pan to tilt in opposite direction. Add white chocolate mousse to the other side of the loaf pan. Chill until firm, for about 1 hour.
- Milk-chocolate layer: in saucepan over low heat, stir milk chocolate, butter and raspberry puree until smooth. Cool slightly, then fold in whipped cream with a spatula. Level the loaf pan. Add mousse over top, covering the dark and milk layers. At this point you don't need to support the loaf pan anymore. Cover the cake with the clear plastic wrap and smooth out the top. Refrigerate until firm, about 2 hours.
- Meanwhile, make the raspberry sauce: In food processor, puree thawed raspberries; strain into small saucepan so that there are no seeds. Stir cornstarch and sugar into puree. Bring to a low boil, stirring. Simmer 1 minute. Cool, refrigerate until serving.
- When the cake is firm, unmold it on a large plate, carefully remove the plastic wrap.

- When ready to serve, arrange a fork and a spoon on a plate. Dust with cocoa, remove utensils. This will make an imprint of the fork and spoon on the plate. This step is totally optional. Slice the mousse cake on the plate and drizzle some raspberry sauce.

190. Tofu Chocolate Mousse Recipe

Serving: 6 | Prep: | Cook: | Ready in:

Ingredients

- 1 lb firm, silken tofu
- 1 cup honey
- 3/4 cup unsweetened cocoa powder
- 1/2 tsp vanilla extract
- 6 strawberries

Direction

- In a food processor whip the tofu until smooth.
- Add the honey, cocoa, and vanilla.
- Blend until well combined.
- Divide among serving glasses and chill for 2 hrs. Garnish with a fresh berry.

191. Tofunana Cream Recipe

Serving: 4 | Prep: | Cook: 6hours | Ready in:

Ingredients

- Italian Lady fingers
- (gf: savoyardi, i use dr. Schar's gf lady fingers or make them by myself at home, the next time i'll upload the recipe)
- 300 g medium soft tofu
- 200 g soy yogurt (plain or banana flavored)
- 3 tbsp honey
- 1 large banana, ripe
- 200-300 g strong black fresh made coffee (sweetened or not, to your taste)
- coffee powder for dusting

Direction

- Peel the banana and chop it into a big pieces. Pour them into the food processor. Add the Tofu, the yogurt and the honey. Blend until everything is reduced into a thick creamy consistency. Pour the coffee into a deep dish. Prepare 4 serving cups.
- Fill the bottoms of the cups with 2 tbsp. of the tofu - banana cream. Wet very well one lady finger into the coffee and place it onto the cream. Repeat the same until all ingredients are finished. Sprinkle with some coffee powder or cocoa powder, or melted dark chocolate and transfer into the refrigerator. Chill at least 4-6 hours, before serving.

192. Triple Chocolate Overload Mousse Cake Recipe

Serving: 8 | Prep: | Cook: 2hours | Ready in:

Ingredients

- Bottom Layer
- * 6 tbsp unsalted butter (3/4 stick butter)
- * 250g bittersweet chocolate, cut into small cubes
- * 4 large eggs, separated
- * 2 tsp vanilla extract
- * 1 tsp instant espresso coffee
- * pinch of salt
- * 1/3 cup packed light brown sugar
- Middle Layer
- * 2 tbsp Dutch-process cocoa powder
- * 5 tbsp hot water
- * 250g belgium or bittersweet chocolate, cut into small cubes
- * 1-1/2 cups cold heavy cream (1 tetra brick Nestle all purpose cream)
- * 1 tbsp granulated sugar

- * 1 tsp salt
- Top Layer
- * 1 tbsp water
- * ¾ tsp plain powdered gelatin
- * 250g 70% dark chocolate (2 chocolate bars)
- * 1-1/2 cups cold heavy cream (1 tetra brick Nestle all purpose cream)
- * 1/4 cup condensed milk
- * Raspberry jam, chocolate shavings and chocolate praline crunch for garnish (you can also use your favorite fruit compote drizzle)

Direction

- To make the bottom layer
- 1. Preheat oven to 325 F. Grease 9-1/2 inch springform pan and set aside.
- 2. Put butter and chocolate chips to a large heatproof bowl. Set on double boiler with half cup of simmering water. Stir lightly until melted and smooth. Set aside to cool for 5 minutes.
- 3. Meanwhile, combine the egg whites and salt in a medium sized bowl and whisk until frothy. Gradually add half of the brown sugar and whisk until combined. Add the remaining brown sugar and whisk until soft peaks form.
- 4. In a small bowl, mix vanilla and egg yolks. Then slowly pour to the slightly cooled chocolate mixture. Stir until well combined.
- 5. Using whisk, gently fold one third of the egg white mixture into the chocolate batter to lighten it. Add the rest of your egg white mixture and continue folding gently until there are no more white streaks.
- 6. Carefully pour batter into the prepared springform pan. Use a spatula to spread and smooth evenly in pan.
- 7. Bake for about 15-18 minutes, or until the centre of the cake is just set (it'll be soft, but should spring back if gently pressed with your finger.) Set cake aside to cool for 1 hour. Leave it in the pan. It may collapse a bit as it cools.
- To make the middle layer
- 1. Combine cocoa powder and hot water in a small bowl then set aside.
- 2. Melt chocolate chips in a large heatproof bowl set in a double boiler with half cup of simmering water. Stir occasionally until melted and smooth. Remove from heat and let cool for 3 to 5 minutes. Add cocoa powder-water paste to the melted chocolate and mix until smooth.
- 3. In a medium size bowl, whisk heavy cream, sugar, and salt until the mixture begins to thicken. Continue whisking until the mixture forms soft peaks.
- 4. Carefully fold one third of the sweetened whipped cream into the chocolate mixture to lighten it. Add the rest and use a rubber spatula to gently fold the mixture until there are no more white streaks.
- 5. Scoop the mousse to your springform pan, spreading it into an even layer on top of the cooled cake. Gently tap the pan on the counter a few times to remove any large air bubbles. Smooth the top with spatula.
- 6. Wipe up any large drips of mousse from the inside/sides of the pan.
- 7. Refrigerate the cake for at least 15 minutes while you make the top layer.
- To make the top layer
- 1. In a small bowl, dissolve gelatine powder in water. Set aside for 5 minutes.
- 2. Melt dark chocolate in a large heatproof bowl set in a double boiler with half cup of simmering water. Gradually add ½ cup of the heavy cream and condensed milk. Stir occasionally until well combined.
- 3. Remove the pan from heat and whisk in the gelatine mixture until it is completely dissolved. Set aside to cool for about 5 minutes, stirring every few minutes to keep the mixture liquid/smooth.
- 4. Whisk the remaining cup of heavy cream in a medium sized bowl until cream begins to thicken. Continue to beat until the mixture forms soft peaks.
- 5. Carefully fold one third of the whipped cream into the dark chocolate mixture to lighten it. Add the rest of the whipped cream and use a rubber spatula to gently fold the mixture until there are no more white streaks.

- 6. Spoon the dark chocolate mousse onto the middle layer. With an offset spatula, spread evenly and smooth top layer.
- 7. Refrigerate the cake until set, at least 2 1/2 hours to overnight.
- 8. Garnish the cake with chocolate shavings, chocolate praline crunch and fruit compote drizzle before serving.
- 9. Run a thin knife between the cake and the sides of the springform pan before removing the pan. To keep your layers clean with each slice, use clean warm knife between slices.
- 10. Enjoy the triple chocolate overload mousse cake!

193. Triple Chocolate Mousse Cake Recipe

Serving: 8 | Prep: | Cook: 20mins | Ready in:

Ingredients

- vegetable-oil cooking spray
- ⅔ cup all-purpose flour
- ⅓ cup unsweetened Dutch-process cocoa powder
- ⅔ cup sugar
- ½ teaspoon baking soda
- ¾ teaspoon baking powder
- ¼ teaspoon salt
- 1 large egg, room temperature
- ¼ cup whole milk
- 3 tablespoons vegetable oil
- ½ teaspoon pure vanilla extract
- Individual chocolate Mousse
- 2 ounces solid semisweet chocolate
- Individual chocolate Mousse:Makes enough for 8 cakes
- 3 ⅓ cups heavy cream
- 8 large egg yolks, room temperature
- ½ cup sugar
- ¼ cup light corn syrup
- 7 ounces bittersweet chocolate, melted
- 2 teaspoons pure vanilla extract
- salt
- 7 ounces milk chocolate, melted

Direction

- Recipe by way of Martha Stewart
- Individual Chocolate Mousse:
- 1. Put 1 ⅔ cups cream into the bowl of an electric mixer fitted with the whisk attachment; beat on medium-high speed until soft peaks form, about 3 ½ minutes. Transfer to a bowl; refrigerate 1 hour.
- 2. Put 4 egg yolks into the clean bowl of the mixer fitted with the clean whisk attachment; beat on high speed until pale and frothy, 4 to 5 minutes. Meanwhile, bring ¼ cup sugar, 2 tablespoons corn syrup, and 2 tablespoons water to a rolling boil in a small, heavy saucepan over high heat. Cook until clear, large bubbles form, about 1 minute. Reduce mixer speed to medium-low. Carefully pour hot syrup down side of bowl. Raise speed to medium-high. Mix until slightly thickened, about 5 minutes. Stir in bittersweet chocolate, 1 teaspoon vanilla, and a pinch of salt with a rubber spatula.
- 3. Add one-third of bittersweet-chocolate mixture to whipped cream; whisk to combine. Add remaining bittersweet-chocolate mixture, whisking until completely combined. Press through a large-mesh sieve into a large bowl; discard any solids. Repeat entire recipe, substituting milk chocolate for the bittersweet.
- Mousse Cakes:
- 1. Preheat oven to 350 degrees. Place eight 6-ounce (3 ½-inch diameter) ramekins on a rimmed baking sheet, and coat with cooking spray; set aside.
- 2. Stir flour, cocoa powder, sugar, baking soda, baking powder, and salt in the bowl of an electric mixer. Attach bowl to mixer fitted with the paddle attachment. Add egg, milk, oil, vanilla, and ¼ cup water; mix on medium-low speed until smooth and combined, about 3 minutes.
- 3. Divide batter evenly among prepared ramekins. Bake until a cake tester inserted into

the centres comes out clean, about 20 minutes. Transfer to a wire rack; let cool completely. Run a knife around sides of cakes; unmould. Cakes can be refrigerated, wrapped in plastic, up to 1 day.

- 4. Trim each cake to 1 inch high. Transfer to a baking sheet lined with parchment paper. Cut eight 10 ¾-by-4-inch strips of parchment paper. Wrap a parchment collar around base of each cake, keeping bottom flush with baking sheet. Secure each collar with tape; set aside.
- 5. Transfer bittersweet-chocolate mousse to a large pastry bag fitted with a large round tip (such as Ateco #808). Pipe a 1-inch layer of mousse into each parchment collar. Refrigerate until mousse is set, about 20 minutes. Repeat with milk chocolate mousse, piping on top of the bittersweet chocolate mousse. Refrigerate at least 4 hours and up to overnight.
- 6. Microwave semisweet chocolate until slightly warm but not melted, about 30 seconds. Scrape at a 45-degree angle with a vegetable peeler, forming curls. Before serving cakes, remove parchment collars, and garnish with chocolate curls.

194. Triple Chocolate Mousse Cake Recipe

Serving: 12 | Prep: | Cook: 40mins | Ready in:

Ingredients

- Bottom Layer
- 6 tablespoons (3/4 stick) unsalted butter, cut into 6 pieces, plus extra for greasing pan
- 7 ounces, chopped fine bittersweet chocolate (Ghirardelli Bittersweet)
- 3/4 teaspoon instant espresso powder
- 1 1/2 teaspoons vanilla extract
- 4 large eggs, separated
- Pinch table salt
- 1/3 cup packed (about 2 1/2 ounces) light brown sugar, crumbled with fingers to remove lumps
- Middle Layer
- 2 tablespoons cocoa powder, preferably Dutch-processed
- 5 tablespoons hot water
- 7 ounces, chopped fine bittersweet chocolate (Ghirardelli Bittersweet)
- 1 1/2 cups cold heavy cream
- 1 tablespoon granulated sugar
- 1/8 teaspoon table salt
- Top Layer
- 3/4 teaspoon powdered gelatin
- 1 tablespoon water
- 6 ounces white chocolate chips (Guittard Choc-Au-Lait)
- 1 1/2 cups cold heavy cream
- Shaved chocolate or cocoa powder for serving, optional

Direction

- FOR THE BOTTOM LAYER: Adjust oven rack to middle position and heat oven to 325 degrees. Butter bottom and sides of 91/2-inch spring form pan. Melt butter, chocolate, and espresso powder in large heatproof bowl set over saucepan filled with 1 inch of barely simmering water, stirring occasionally until smooth. Remove from heat and cool mixture slightly, about 5 minutes. Whisk in vanilla and egg yolks; set aside.
- In stand mixer fitted with whisk attachment, beat egg whites and salt at medium speed until frothy, about 30 seconds. Add half of brown sugar and beat until combined, about 15 seconds. Add remaining brown sugar and beat at high speed until soft peaks form when whisk is lifted, about 1 minute longer, scraping down sides halfway through. Using whisk, fold one-third of beaten egg whites into chocolate mixture to lighten. Using rubber spatula, fold in remaining egg whites until no white streaks remain. Carefully transfer batter to prepared springform pan, gently smoothing top with offset spatula.

- Bake until cake has risen, is firm around edges, and centre has just set but is still soft (centre of cake will spring back after pressing gently with finger), 13 to 18 minutes. Transfer cake to wire rack to cool completely, about 1 hour. (Cake will collapse as it cools.) Do not remove cake from pan.
- FOR THE MIDDLE LAYER: Combine cocoa powder and hot water in small bowl; set aside. Melt chocolate in large heatproof bowl set over saucepan filled with 1 inch of barely simmering water, stirring occasionally until smooth. Remove from heat and cool slightly, 2 to 5 minutes.
- In clean bowl of stand mixer fitted with whisk attachment, whip cream, granulated sugar, and salt at medium speed until mixture begins to thicken, about 30 seconds. Increase speed to high and whip until soft peaks form when whisk is lifted, 15 to 60 seconds.
- Whisk cocoa powder mixture into melted chocolate until smooth. Using whisk, fold one-third of whipped cream into chocolate mixture to lighten. Using rubber spatula, fold in remaining whipped cream until no white streaks remain. Spoon mousse into springform pan over cooled cake and gently tap pan on counter 3 times to remove any large air bubbles; gently smooth top with offset spatula. Wipe inside edge of pan with damp cloth to remove any drips. Refrigerate cake at least 15 minutes while preparing top layer.
- FOR THE TOP LAYER: In small bowl, sprinkle gelatine over water; let stand at least 5 minutes. Place white chocolate in medium bowl. Bring ½ cup cream to simmer in small saucepan over medium-high heat. Remove from heat; add gelatine mixture and stir until fully dissolved. Pour cream mixture over white chocolate and whisk until chocolate is melted and mixture is smooth, about 30 seconds. Cool to room temperature, stirring occasionally, 5 to 8 minutes (mixture will thicken slightly).
- In clean bowl of stand mixer fitted with whisk attachment, whip remaining cup cream at medium speed until it begins to thicken, about 30 seconds. Increase speed to high and whip until soft peaks form when whisk is lifted, 15 to 60 seconds. Using whisk, fold one-third of whipped cream into white chocolate mixture to lighten. Using rubber spatula, fold remaining whipped cream into white chocolate mixture until no white streaks remain. Spoon white chocolate mousse into pan over middle layer. Smooth top with offset spatula. Return cake to refrigerator and chill until set, at least 2½ hours.
- TO SERVE: If using, garnish top of cake with chocolate curls or dust with cocoa. Run thin knife between cake and side of springform pan; remove side of pan. Run cleaned knife along outside of cake to smooth sides. Cut into slices and serve.

195. Two Whiskey Chocolate Mousse Recipe

Serving: 6 | Prep: | Cook: 10mins | Ready in:

Ingredients

- 1/4 cup boiling water
- 1 TBSP. dark roasted, ground coffee
- 4 ounces unsweetened chocolate
- 1/4 teasp. salt
- 1/3 cup plus 1 cup heavy cream
- 2 TBSP. butter
- 8 - 10 TBSP. sugar.(depends on how sweet you want it)
- 1 teasp. vanilla
- 1 TBSP. bourbon
- 1 TBSP. dark rum

Direction

- Pour the boiling water over the ground coffee.
- Let steep for a minute or two....strain
- In a double boiler put the chocolate, salt, 1/3 cup of cream and the butter and the coffee flavored water

- Melt the chocolate and stir until smooth... let cool to lukewarm
- Whip the 1 cup of cream, adding the sugar slowly, until stiff peaks form
- Fold the flavourings into the whipped cream
- Fold the whipped cream into the melted chocolate
- Makes about 5 cups

196. Utah Strawberry Chocolate Mousse Recipe

Serving: 8 | Prep: | Cook: 10mins | Ready in:

Ingredients

- 1 pound fresh strawberries
- 1 envelope unflavored gelatin
- 1/4 cup cold water
- 1/2 cup milk
- 1/3 cup cocoa
- 1/3 cup granulated sugar
- 1/2 teaspoon pure vanilla extract
- 1 cup whipping cream

Direction

- Wash drain and core strawberries.
- In blender container sprinkle gelatine over water then allow standing 5 minutes to soften.
- Heat milk until hot but do not boil then add to the gelatine mixture.
- Process on low speed until gelatine granules are dissolved scraping sides of blender.
- Add cocoa and sugar then blend until sugar is dissolved.
- Add strawberries and vanilla and blend well.
- Add whipping cream and blend well then pour into dessert dishes.
- Cover and refrigerate until serving time.

197. Valentine Parfait White Chocolate Mousse With Red Raspberry Coulis Recipe

Serving: 48 | Prep: | Cook: 15mins | Ready in:

Ingredients

- RASPBERRY SAUCE
- 2 10-ounce packages frozen raspberries in syrup
- juice of 1/2 lemon
- 1/4 cup sugar
- 2 tablespoons cornstarch
- 1/2 cup water
- 1 tablespoon Grand Marnier or other liqueur (optional)
- MOUSE
- 1/4 cup water
- 1 teaspoon unflavored gelatin
- 1/4 cup milk
- 5 ounces white chocolate** -- broken up
- 1 1/2 cups heavy whipping cream

Direction

- Combine undrained berries and lemon juice in processor or blender and puree. Strain, pressing with back of spoon. Add sugar, cornstarch, water and liqueur; blend well.
- Place in saucepan over medium heat and bring to boil, stirring frequently. Reduce heat and continue stirring one minute. Remove from heat and allow to cool until ready to use.
- In a glass measuring cup, sprinkle gelatin over cold water and allow mixture to soften for 1-2 minutes. Microwave on HIGH 20-40 seconds and allow to stand for 2 minutes, or until granules are completely dissolved. (Alternatively, place cup in a bowl of hot water and stir until completely dissolved.)
- In a small saucepan bring milk to the simmering point. Remove from heat and add white chocolate. Stir occasionally until chocolate is melted and mixture is smooth. Blend gelatin into chocolate mixture and

refrigerate until slightly thickened but not gelled - about 10 minutes.
- Whip cream until stiff and peaks hold their shape. Fold white chocolate mixture into whipped cream. Beginning with raspberry sauce, alternate layers of mousse with raspberry sauce into tall parfait glasses. Refrigerate 1-2 hours. To serve, garnish with partially frozen whole berries, or fresh if available.

198. Valentines Day Chocolate Mousse Recipe

Serving: 8 | Prep: | Cook: 35mins | Ready in:

Ingredients

- 12-ounce pkg (1-3/4 cups) semisweet chocolate chips
- 1 C milk or half and half
- 1-1/2 C Imperial sugar Granulated sugar or Dixie Crystals Granulated sugar
- 4 eggs, lightly beaten
- 1/4 C liqueur (brandy, Kahlua, Amaretto, Grand Marnier)
- 3 C heavy cream
- sweetened whipped cream, for garnish
- grated chocolate or chocolate curls, for garnish
- --------------------
- HEART SHAPED DISHES FROM TARGET

Direction

- Melt chocolate chips in the top half of a double boiler over hot, but not simmering water.
- Scald milk with 1 cup of the sugar until dissolved.
- Do not boil.
- Slowly stir hot milk mixture into the melted chocolate.
- Stir until smooth with a wire whisk at all times.
- Beat eggs lightly and slowly pour into the chocolate mixture stirring vigorously with the whisk at all times.
- Cook mixture, stirring constantly with the whisk until thick and creamy, about 20 minutes.
- Keep water in the bottom half of the double boiler just below a simmer.
- Thickened mixture will have the consistency of chocolate pudding. Remove from heat and stir in your choice of liqueur.
- Cool to room temperature.
- Do not chill.
- Add the remaining 1/2 cup of sugar to the heavy cream and beat until stiff.
- Fold the chocolate mixture into the whipped cream until thoroughly blended.
- Spoon mixture into a large (about 6 cups) crystal serving bowl. Cover and chill until firm, at least one hour.
- Garnish mousse with sweetened whipped cream and grated or curled chocolate.

199. WISCONSIN MASCARPONE MOUSSE WITH HAZELNUT DESSERT Recipe

Serving: 6 | Prep: | Cook: | Ready in:

Ingredients

- 1 pound Wisconsin mascarpone cheese
- 1 1/2 ounces pasteurized egg yolk product (equivalent of 3 egg yolks)
- 2/3 cup sugar
- 1/2 cup hazelnut liqueur
- 6 ounces pasteurized egg white product (equivalent of 5 egg whites)
- 1 cup chopped, toasted hazelnuts
- mint sprigs, for garnish

Direction

- In a large bowl, beat cheese, egg yolk product, sugar and liqueur until light and airy.
- In another bowl, whip egg white product until stiff. Gently fold egg whites into cheese mixture. Pour into individual ramekins or stemmed glasses. Sprinkle with hazelnuts. Refrigerate several hours. Garnish with fresh mint sprigs

200. Whisky Mousse Recipe

Serving: 4 | Prep: | Cook: 5mins | Ready in:

Ingredients

- 100 grs plain chocolate
- 2 gelatine sheets (unflavoured)
- 2 eggs
- 50 grs confectioner's sugar
- 50 grs white chocolate
- 0.5 dl whisky
- Grated chocolate.

Direction

- Melt the plain chocolate.
- With the help of a pastry brush coat the insides of muffin-size paper cases.
- Put in the freezer for a few minutes.
- Remove from the freezer and repeat the coating procedure.
- Put back in the freezer.
- Soak the gelatine in cold water.
- Whisk the egg yolks with the sugar.
- Melt the white chocolate and gelatine together.
- Add to the yolks
- Add the egg whites previously whisked to soft-peak.
- Carefully peel off the paper cases.
- Fill the chocolate cases with the mousse.
- Sprinkle with the grated chocolate and chill.

201. White Chocolate Coconut Mousse Recipe

Serving: 4 | Prep: | Cook: 15mins | Ready in:

Ingredients

- 1 oz. bittersweet chocolate, melted
- 1-1/2 c (1%) low-fat milk
- 1 pkg (1oz.) instant sugar-free, fat-free white - chocolate pudding mix
- 1/4 tsp coconut extract
- 2 c thawed reduced-fat frozen whipped topping
- toasted coconut and chocolate-dipped almonds, optional

Direction

- Transfer melted chocolate to small plastic food storage bag; snip small hole in one corner. Decoratively pipe chocolate onto insides of 4 (6oz each) glass serving dishes.
- Refrigerate till chocolate has set, about 5 mins.
- Meanwhile, in large bowl, whisk together milk, dry pudding mix and extract till thick and smooth, 1-2 mins. Fold in whipped topping; divide among prepared dishes.
- Refrigerate till well chilled and set, about 1 hr. If desired, serve sprinkled with coconut and almonds.

202. White Chocolate Lime Mousse Recipe

Serving: 6 | Prep: | Cook: 10mins | Ready in:

Ingredients

- 1-1/2 teaspoons unflavored gelatin
- 2 tablespoons cold water
- 8 ounces white chocolate chopped
- 2/3 cup heavy cream
- 5 tablespoons lime juice
- Rind of 1 lime grated

- 2 egg whites
- 1/8 teaspoon salt
- 2 teaspoons superfine sugar
- lime zest to decorate

Direction

- Sprinkle gelatine over water in a cup and leave for 5 minutes to turn spongy.
- Put cup in a bowl of hot water and let gelatine dissolve.
- Carefully melt chocolate in a double boiler.
- Whip cream until it forms soft peaks.
- Stir a large spoonful of cream into chocolate.
- Add gelatine, lime juice and rind then fold in remaining cream.
- Whisk egg whites with salt until they form soft peaks then add sugar and whisk 30 seconds more.
- Fold a large spoonful of egg whites into chocolate then fold in remaining whites.
- Spoon mixture into 6 ramekins and chill 6 hours.
- Garnish with lime zest and serve.

203. White Chocolate Mousse

Serving: 2 | Prep: | Cook: 5mins | Ready in:

Ingredients

- 1 cup heavy whipping cream
- 2 tablespoons sugar
- 3 ounces cream cheese, softened
- 3 ounces white baking chocolate, melted and cooled
- 2 cups blueberries, raspberries or strawberries
- Additional berries, optional

Direction

- In a bowl, beat cream until it begins to thicken. Gradually add sugar, beating until stiff peaks form; set aside.
- In another bowl, beat cream cheese until fluffy. Add chocolate and beat until smooth.
- Fold in whipped cream. Alternate layers of mousse and berries in parfait glasses, ending with mousse. Garnish with additional berries if desired. Serve immediately or refrigerate for up to 3 hours.

204. White Chocolate Mousse In Milk Chocolate Shells Recipe

Serving: 8 | Prep: | Cook: 240mins | Ready in:

Ingredients

- Mousse
- 4 1/2 oz. white chocolate baking bar, cut up
- 1 1/2 cups whipping cream
- 3/4 teaspoon vanilla
- Shells
- 1 (7-oz.) bar milk chocolate, cut up
- 1 tablespoon oil

Direction

- DIRECTIONS
- 1. In small saucepan, combine white chocolate baking bar and whipping cream; heat over low heat, stirring constantly until baking bar is melted and smooth.
- 2. Stir in vanilla. Pour into small bowl; cover with plastic wrap. Refrigerate 4 hours or overnight until mixture is very cold and thickened, stirring occasionally.
- 3. Line 8 muffin cups with foil or paper baking cups. In small saucepan, combine milk chocolate and oil; heat over low heat, stirring until chocolate is melted and smooth. Remove from heat.
- 4. With small paint brush, pastry brush or teaspoon, brush thin layer of chocolate evenly over sides and bottom of each foil cup. Place in freezer until firm, about 5 minutes. Repeat coating process of cups using remaining

chocolate. Place in freezer until firm, 10 to 20 minutes.
- 5. Carefully peel foil cups from chocolate shells; place shells in refrigerator while preparing filling. With electric mixer, beat white chocolate mixture at high speed until light and fluffy. DO NOT OVERBEAT.
- 6. To serve, spoon 1/2 cup mousse into each chocolate shell. If desired, garnish with stemmed maraschino cherry. Store in refrigerator.

205. White Chocolate Mousse Recipe

Serving: 6 | Prep: | Cook: 360mins | Ready in:

Ingredients

- 1 cup 30% whipping cream
- 5 1/2 oz high quality white chocolate
- 1 1/2 oz white sugar
- 3 1/2 oz unsalted butter
- 9 egg whites
- 3 egg yolks
- 1/2 oz whiskey (rye or bourbon)
- For garnish : white chocolate curls, fresh raspberries or blueberries, mint leaves ... use your imagination

Direction

- In first bowl, beat egg yolks with sugar until glistening, white in colour and smooth. Set aside.
- In another bowl, whip cream, gradually adding whiskey, until stiff. Set aside.
- Melt chocolate and butter GENTLY together in a double boiler over LOW heat. I use a glass bowl over barely simmering water; remove it completely from the heat before the chocolate has completely melted, and continue stirring until smooth and incorporated. Set aside.
- In a separate bowl, whip egg whites until very stiff. Set aside.

206. White Chocolate Mousse Tarts Recipe

Serving: 12 | Prep: | Cook: 30mins | Ready in:

Ingredients

- 6 oz white baking chocolate,chopped
- 1 can (14 oz) sweetened condensed milk
- 1/4 tsp vanilla
- 2 c heavy whipping cream,whipped
- 2 pkgs (6 ct. ea) individual graham cracker tart shells
- assorted fresh fruit,optional

Direction

- In a microwave, melt chocolate; stir till smooth. Transfer to large bowl; whisk in milk and vanilla. Fold in whipped cream. Spoon into tart shells. Garnish with fruit, if desired. Chill till serving.

207. White Chocolate Mousse With Fresh Raspberry Sauce Recipe

Serving: 6 | Prep: | Cook: 300mins | Ready in:

Ingredients

- Mousse:
- 3 TBSP. Cold water
- ¾ tsp. plain unflavored gelatin (⅓ envelope)
- 8 oz. white chocolate (1 ⅓ c. white chocolate chips)
- 1 ½ c. heavy cream, divided
- Sauce:
- 1 pint raspberries (or 12 oz. frozen dry-pack raspberries, thawed)
- 3 TBSP. sugar

- 2 tsp. fresh lemon juice

Direction

- * Cook time includes chill time.
- White Chocolate Mousse:
- Have ready six or seven 4 – 6 ounce stemmed glasses or dessert dishes or one 2-quart mold. Lightly oil the mold if you want to turn out the dessert.
- In a small bowl, pour in the cold water. Sprinkle gelatine over the top. Let stand for 5 minutes to soften.
- Very finely chop or in a food processor, grind the white chocolate to a crumb-like consistency. Transfer to a bowl.
- Stirring, bring to a boil in a small saucepan ½ cup of the heavy cream. Remove from the heat, add the softened gelatine, and stir for 30 seconds to dissolve the gelatine granules. Immediately pour this mixture over the chocolate and whisk until smooth.
- Refrigerate the chocolate mixture until cold and thick enough to fall from a spoon in heavy, satiny ribbons, 15 to 45 minutes.
- Beat on medium-high speed until stiff enough to hold a firm shape on a spoon the remaining 1 cup of heavy cream. Fold a small amount of the cream into the chocolate mixture to lighten it. Then carefully fold the remaining whipped cream in the chocolate mixture.
- Turn into the glasses, dishes, or mold and refrigerate for 2 hours, or at least 4 hours if unmolding. Serve with Raspberry Coulis and a sprig of mint.
- Fresh Raspberry Sauce (Raspberry Coulis):
- Puree all ingredients in a blender or food processor.
- Strain mixture through a fine-mesh sieve, into a bowl, pressing firmly with a rubber spatula. Press firmly and periodically scrape the inside of the sieve clear of seeds, which will otherwise plug up the holes. Do not waste the pulp. Continue to press until you are left with just a heaping tablespoon of the stiff, clumped together seeds.
- Taste, then stir in a little more sugar or lemon juice if needed. Serve at once, or cover and refrigerate for up to 3 days.

208. White Chocolate Mousse With Raspberry Swirl Recipe

Serving: 8 | Prep: | Cook: 10mins | Ready in:

Ingredients

- 1 tablespoon cold water
- 1/2 teaspoon unflavored gelatin
- 1/2 cup heavy whipping cream
- 3 ounces white chocolate
- 1/4 cup pureed raspberries
- 15 miniature phyllo cups
- 1/4 cup halved raspberries for garnish

Direction

- In a small pan combine water and gelatine then allow to stand 1 minute to soften.
- Add 2 tablespoons of heavy cream then stir over low heat until gelatine dissolves.
- Add white chocolate and stir until melted.
- Chill until cool but not set about 10 minutes.
- In a small chilled bowl whip remaining heavy cream to full volume.
- Fold whipped cream into cooled chocolate.
- Drizzle pureed raspberries onto cooled chocolate.
- Run a knife through chocolate to create raspberry swirls.
- Chill for 1 hour.
- Spoon or pipe 2 teaspoons of filling into each shell then garnish with raspberry half.
- Serve immediately.

209. White Chocolate Mousse With Strawberries Recipe

Serving: 6 | Prep: | Cook: | Ready in:

Ingredients

- 2 cups fresh strawberries*, stems removed
- 1/4 cup granulated sugar
- 1 tbsp. kirsch (clear cherry brandy) or framboise (raspberry liqueur)
- 6 oz. white chocolate, finely chopped
- 1/4 cup milk, warmed
- 1 cup heavy cream
- 2 egg whites, at room temperature
- Pinch of cream of tartar
- 3/4 tsp. vanilla extract

Direction

- In a blender or in a food processor fitted with the metal blade, combine 1 1/2 cups of the strawberries with the sugar.
- Puree until smooth.
- Strain through a fine-mesh sieve into a bowl.
- Add the kirsch and stir to mix.
- Cut the remaining 1/2 cup strawberries lengthwise into thin slices and stir into the puree.
- Set aside.
- Place the chocolate in a heatproof bowl set over a pan of gently simmering water; do not allow the bowl to touch the water.
- Heat the chocolate, stirring occasionally, until it is melted and smooth and registers 140°F on an instant-read thermometer.
- Gradually add the warm milk to the chocolate, stirring constantly until smooth.
- Remove the bowl from the pan of water and let the mixture cool until it is almost at room temperature.
- In a bowl, using an electric mixer on high speed, beat the cream just until soft peaks form. In another bowl, using clean beaters, beat together the egg whites and cream of tartar on high speed until stiff peaks form.
- Using a rubber spatula, fold half of the whites into the chocolate mixture to lighten it.
- Fold the remaining whites, whipped cream and vanilla into the chocolate mixture just until combined and no white drifts remain. Do not over mix. (At this point, you may cover and refrigerate the mousse for up to 1 day).
- To serve, spoon about half of the mousse into 6 parfait glasses, half filling each glass.
- Top with the strawberry sauce, again using about half and dividing it equally. Repeat with the remaining mousse and strawberry sauce.

210. White Chocolate Raspberry Mousse Recipe

Serving: 6 | Prep: | Cook: 15mins | Ready in:

Ingredients

- 12 oz white chocolate, chopped
- 1/2 tsp gelatin powder
- 1/2 cup milk
- 1 cup whipping cream
- 3 tbsp. Chambord (raspberry liqueur)
- 1 cup raspberries

Direction

- Melt chocolate in a bowl resting over a pot of gently simmering water, stirring constantly.
- Heat milk (microwave is easiest) to just below a simmer and sprinkle with gelatine, allow to sit for 1 minute.
- Then, whisk milk and gelatine mixture into chocolate. Let cool to room temperature.
- Whip cream to soft peaks and fold in Chambord. Fold whipped cream into chocolate.
- Sprinkle the raspberries into the mousse mixture and gently fold.
- Pour in to glasses and chill for at least 4 hours before serving.

- SERVING: I like to serve it in a martini glass with a raspberry and chocolate shaving for garnish

211. White Chocolate Grand Marnier Mousse In Chocolate Pistachio Tuile Cups Recipe

Serving: 6 | Prep: | Cook: 25mins | Ready in:

Ingredients

- 4 large egg yolks
- 1/4 cup Grand Marnier
- 2 tablespoons granulated sugar
- 1 tablespoon grated orange zest
- 2 cups unsweetened whipped cream
- 1/2 cup melted white chocolate
- chocolate-Pistachio Tuile Cups, recipe follows

Direction

- In a stainless steel bowl set over a saucepan of boiling water, combine the egg yolks, Grand Marnier, sugar, and orange zest, and whisk to incorporate. Whisking constantly and removing from the heat from time to time, cook until the mixture has thickened and coats the back of a spoon into a sabayon, 4 to 5 minutes. Remove from the heat and cool.
- Fold the whipped cream into the cooled sabayon, then fold in the melted chocolate. Refrigerate until well chilled, at least 6 hours. Transfer to a pastry bag fitted with a star tip.
- To serve, place 1 tuile cup in the centre of 8 dessert plates. Pipe (or alternately spoon) 1/4 cup of the mousse into the cups and garnish with the mint sprigs and powdered sugar. Serve.
- Chocolate-Pistachio Tuile Cups:
- 2 large egg whites
- 4 tablespoons plus 2 teaspoons granulated sugar
- 5 tablespoons butter, melted
- 1/2 teaspoon vanilla extract
- 5 tablespoons plus 1 teaspoon all-purpose flour
- 1 tablespoon plus 1 teaspoon cocoa powder
- 4 teaspoons crushed pistachios
- Preheat oven to 350 degrees F. Line a large baking sheet with parchment paper and set aside. Invert 8 shot glasses or tea cups on the counter.
- In a medium bowl, whisk together the egg whites, sugar, and pistachios until just combined. Add the butter and vanilla, and whisk. Add the flour and cocoa powder, and whisk. Drop the batter by 1 1/2 tablespoonfuls onto the baking sheet, about 4 inches apart. Using a small spatula or the back of a spoon, spread the batter out to form a thin 4 1/2 -inch circle (the batter needs to be a thin, even coat because the cookies will not spread when cooked). Bake for 12 to 13 minutes, or until a deep brown. Remove from the oven.
- With a thin spatula, quickly remove the cookies 1 at a time from the baking sheet and drape on top of a ramekin to create a cup shape. (If the cookies become too brittle, replace on the baking sheet and place in the oven for 10 seconds to soften.) Cool completely on the glasses, then gently lift off and transfer to a platter until ready to use. Yield: 8 cookies

212. White Milk And Dark Chocolate Mousse Recipe

Serving: 12 | Prep: | Cook: 12mins | Ready in:

Ingredients

- white chocolate MOUSSE
- 9 oz. white chocolate
- 1 ½ tsp. unflavored gelatin
- 5 Tbsp. water
- 1 Tbsp. light corn syrup
- 2 egg yolks
- 1/3 cup whipping cream

- 2/3 cup dairy sour cream
- milk chocolate MOUSSE
- 6 oz. milk chocolate
- ¼ cup strong coffee
- 2 tsp. unflavored gelatin
- 3 Tbsp. water
- 8 Tbsp. butter
- 2 egg yolks
- 1 ¼ cups whipping cream
- DECORATION
- chocolate GANACHE
- 9 1/2 oz. dark chocolate
- 1 1/2oz. heavy cream
- 1 Tbsp. butter.
- ISOMALT sugar DECORATIONS
- 1.000 gr. Isomalt sugar
- 8 gr. water

Direction

- Line round pan with a plastic wrap, the best you can.
- WHITE CHOCOLATE MOUSSE
- Break chocolate in small pieces and set aside.
- In small bowl sprinkle gelatine unflavoured gratin over 3 Tablespoons of water, put it in the microwave for 20 sec.
- In a saucepan combine remaining water and corn syrup and bring to a boil, remove from heat and stir in gelatine, until perfectly dissolved.
- Add chocolate pieces and beat until chocolate is melted and mixture smooth.
- Beat in egg yolks 1 at the time.
- In a bowl whip whipping cream and sour cream lightly, and fold into chocolate mixture.
- Pour into prepared mould and refrigerate until set.
- MILK CHOCOLATE MOUSSE
- Melt chocolate with coffee, if you like in the microwave or in top of a double boiler or bowl set over a pan of simmering water.
- Sprinkle gelatine over water, mix it and put it in the microwave for 20 sec. then stir gelatine into chocolate and then add the butter, until it is melted and the mix is smooth.
- Then cool and beat in the egg yolks.
- In a bowl, whip cream lightly and fold into chocolate mixture.
- Pour milk chocolate over set white chocolate mousse.
- Refrigerate until set, then cover with overlapping plastic wrap and refrigerate overnight.
- Next day
- Prepare dark chocolate Ganache by heating the heavy cream and adding the dark chocolate in little pieces, then finally the melted butter.
- Let it stand and cool.
- Take out the chocolate mousse and carefully peel the plastic wrap
- Cover it with the ganache and refrigerate again.
- ISOMALT DECORATIONS
- This method is a little elaborated I only took some isomalt sugar and put it in the microwave only a few seconds then again and again until melted, then put it in silicone paper and with a glass cup just try to make decorations, you can look for detailed explanations here:

213. White Chocolate Mousse Recipe

Serving: 8 | Prep: | Cook: 30mins | Ready in:

Ingredients

- 400gr white chocolate.
- 600 gr heavy cream.
- 100 gr haselnuts halved, (optional).
- 1 1/2 shredded lemon peel or 1 shredded orange peel.

Direction

- Cut white chocolate in little pieces with a knife or in the blender.

- Beat the heavy cream till you have a thick cream, (take care not to beat it till whipped cream)!
- Melt de white chocolate in a Choco pan or au Bain Marie.
- Take away from heat and let cool down till lukewarm.
- Mix de cream, shredded lemon or orange peel and hazelnuts carefully with the chocolate till you have a smooth mass.
- Fill 8 glasses or desert bowls and put minimum 2 hours in the fridge, (you can make this the day before and keep in the fridge till use).
- Serve with lemon or orange parts and top if you wish with a dark chocolate sauce or a little cocoa or cinnamon.

214. Wildly Chocolate Brownies With Mousse Topping Recipe

Serving: 16 | Prep: | Cook: 27mins | Ready in:

Ingredients

- Brownie:
- ·1 cup sugar
- ·2 eggs
- ·½ tsp. vanilla extract
- ·½ cup butter or margarine, melted
- ·½ cup all-purpose flour
- ·1/3 cup baking cocoa
- ·¼ tsp. baking powder
- ·¼ tsp. salt
- Frosting:
- ·¾ cup semisweet chocolate chips
- ·3 tbs. water
- ·1 tbs. butter
- ·¾ cup heavy whipping cream, whipped

Direction

- For brownie base, in a large mixing bowl, beat sugar, eggs and vanilla.
- Add butter; mix well.
- Combine dry ingredients; add to batter and mix well.
- Pour into a foil-lined 8-in. square-baking pan.
- Bake at 350 for 25-30 minutes or until brownies test done with a toothpick inserted halfway to the centre of the pan.
- Cool pan on wire rack.
- For frosting, melt chocolate chips, water, and butter in a microwave or double boiler; stir until smooth.
- Cool to room temperature.
- Fold in whipped cream.
- Spread over brownies.
- Chill before cutting.
- Wet knife between cuts for a cleaner look.
- Store in the refrigerator.

215. Wills Chocolate Mousse Recipe

Serving: 16 | Prep: | Cook: 13mins | Ready in:

Ingredients

- 1 qt. WHOLE REAL CREAM
- 1 package yogurt starter
- 1/4 c. Undutched cocoa
- 1 oz. Unsweet chocolate
- 1 package Unflavored geletain (optional)
- 1 3/4 c. brown sugar
- 2 chocolate pie crusts (optional)

Direction

- SLOWLY Warm the cream, cocoa, chocolate, (optional gelatine if you will not be able to serve frozen, desire a firmer mousse, etc.) Together to 180 degrees and hold for two minutes.
- Cool to 110 degrees, add yogurt starter. incubate in a yogurt maker or a quart jar in water bath (double boiler type setup) at 110 to

114 degrees for 8 to 12 hours (depending on desired tang, longer time = more tangy but you will also have some solid bits of cheese start to form after 8 hours)
- Add the brown sugar stirring slowly until dissolved (but don't whip the cream yet!), refrigerate for 8 hours. If you want a warm mousse you can whip now and serve but you will not get a very firm mousse even with added gelatine warm for obvious reasons.
- Whip to stiff peaks, BE CAREFUL not to over whip.
- You are now ready to serve if bowl is the desired delivery vehicle, spoon into two pie shells or cones, etc., freeze until served.
- NOTES:
- Note: over whipping is not always a bad thing, the butter you separate from the mousse is pretty darned good on its own and the liquid left over is pretty good too!
- Originally designed for my final project for school, and then a friend suggested fermenting the cream and after some experimentation this is the result of that.
- *** You must use whole real dairy cream not the kind you buy in most supermarkets, and un-Dutch (not processed with alkali) or the mouse will not set up correctly.
- The thickeners will cause pockets of goo in the final product or you will have a soup unless you double the gelatine depending on how much of the cream is thickeners.
- The alkali used to lighten cocoa will kill some of the bacteria needed to make the final product awesome and can cause spoiling in some cases.
- Most supermarkets carry un-Dutch or "dark cocoa" cocoa, and health food stores or local small dairies will have real cream. In my area the non-BIG-chain grocers also have cream without the carrageenan or other thickeners.
- Yogurt starter is available in health food stores in freeze dried packets, or you can use LIVE yogurt (1 TB = 1 pack) with no flavouring (some vanilla yogurts will also work but sugar in even small amount can cause problems and will cause major problems in large quantities)

- If you prefer a softer mouse you can keep in the refrigerator however this will not keep as long, and is much harder to handle.
- In the refrigerator it behaves just like whipped cream unless you add the gelatine.
- In the freezer it behaves like ice cream without the gelatine.

216. Yogurt Mousse Recipe

Serving: 4 | Prep: | Cook: | Ready in:

Ingredients

- Yougurt mousse
- 1 cup plain yogurt
- 3 tablespoons sugar
- 1 cup whipped cream
- 2 teaspoons gelatin
- 3 tablespoons hot water

Direction

- Step 1: Mix the yogurt and sugar in a bowl.
- Step 2: In a different bowl, pour whipping cream in and mix until it whips up. Make sure it has the same texture as yogurt.
- Step 3: In a small bowl, put in hot water and pour the gelatine in. Stir as you are pouring the gelatine so it doesn't clump up. Stir until the gelatine is completely melted.
- Step 4: Put the hot water from Step 3 in yogurt and stir immediately. You have to be fast or the gelatine will clump up.
- Step 5: Add the whipped cream from Step 2 into the bowl from Step 4. After mixing them, pour the yogurt into glass cups and chill in the refrigerator for about an hour.
- Step 6: Enjoy!

217. Brownie White Chocolate Mousse Torte Recipe

Serving: 8 | Prep: | Cook: 40mins | Ready in:

Ingredients

- Brownie
- Soft butter for greasing
- 1/4 cup (1/2 stick) butter
- 2 ounces milk chocolate, chopped
- 1 ounce plain chocolate, chopped
- 2 large eggs
- 3/4 cup sugar
- 2 teaspoons vanilla extract
- 1/2 cup cake flour
- Mousse
- 12 ounces good-quality white chocolate (such as Lindt or Baker's), chopped
- 1 1/2 cups chilled whipping cream
- 3 large egg whites
- For garnishing:
- cocoa powder
- 70 grams melted chocolate

Direction

- For brownie:
- Preheat oven to 350°F. Grease 9-inch-diameter springform pan with 2 3/4-inch-high sides with soft butter. Dust pan with flour. Stir butter and both chocolates in heavy small saucepan over low heat until melted and smooth. Cool to room temperature.
- Using electric mixer, beat eggs and sugar in large bowl until thick, about 5 minutes. Beat in vanilla. Stir in chocolate mixture. Sift flour over and fold in. Transfer batter to prepared pan. Bake until tester inserted into center of brownie comes out with dry crumbs attached, about 18 minutes. Cool completely in pan on rack.
- For mousse:
- Stir white chocolate and 3/4 cup cream in heavy medium saucepan over low heat just until white chocolate is melted. Cool completely.
- Beat remaining 3/4 cup cream in another large bowl until peaks form. Using clean dry beaters, beat egg whites in medium bowl until stiff but not dry. Gently fold whites, then whipped cream, into white chocolate mixture. Spoon mousse atop brownie in pan; smooth top. Cover torte and refrigerate overnight.
- For garnishing:
- Sift cocoa powder over torte to cover all surface, then pipe long stripes of melted chocolate over.

218. Chocolate Marshmallow Mousse Recipe

Serving: 6 | Prep: | Cook: 15mins | Ready in:

Ingredients

- 2 cups sugar
- 3/4 cup water
- 1/2 Tbs cornflour
- 1/2 cup water
- 2 heaped Tbs gelatine
- 200 grams plain chocolate{good quality}
- 1 cup milk
- 250 ml fresh cream {whipped}

Direction

- Melt the chocolate and milk together in a double boiler until smooth
- Allow to cool slightly, set aside
- Boil the sugar and water together in a thick based pot on med. heat until a thick and bubbly syrup is formed +- 5 mins /105*C on a sugar thermometer
- In a separate dish mix to the corn flour, water and gelatine until smooth
- Add the hot syrup to the gelatine mixture gradually, using an electric mixer, beat for about 10 mins until thick and sticky
- Add the melted choc and the whipped cream to the marshmallow mix and beat until well combined

- Pour into glass bowls quickly and allow to set
- Decorate with fresh cream rosettes, choc curls and strawberry fans
- YUMMY.....YUMMY......YUMMY.......YUMMY.......YUMMY..........YUMMY.

219. Chocolate Hazelnut Mousse Recipe

Serving: 6 | Prep: | Cook: 30mins | Ready in:

Ingredients

- 1/4 cup sugar
- 1/4 cup unsweetened cocoa
- 2 1/2 tbsp cornstarch
- 1/4 tsp salt
- 2 large eggs
- 2 cups 2% reduced-fat milk
- 1/4 cup Frangelico (hazelnut flavored liqueur)
- 1/2 tsp vanilla extract
- 3 oz bittersweet chocolate chopped
- 2 cups of frozen fat-free whipped topping, thawed
- 2 tbsp chopped hazelnuts, toasted

Direction

- Combine sugar, cocoa, cornstarch, salt and eggs in a medium bowl, stirring well with a whisk
- Heat milk over medium-high heat in a small heavy saucepan to 180 degrees or tiny bubbles form around the edge (do not boil)
- Gradually add hot milk to sugar mixture, stirring constantly with a whisk. Place the milk mixture into pan and cook over medium heat until very thick and bubbly (about 5 min) stirring constantly. Spoon mixture into a medium bowl, add the liqueur, vanilla, and chocolate, stirring until chocolate melts. Place bowl in large ice-filled bowl for 15 min. until mixture is cool, stirring occasionally.
- Remove bowl from ice. Gently fold in one-third of whip topping. Fold remaining topping. Cover and chill at least 3 hours. Sprinkle with hazelnuts. (Serving size about 2/3 cup of mouse and 1 tsp. hazelnuts)
- Calories 278 (30% from fat) FAT 9.2 g (sat 4.4g) mono 3.5 g poly .05 g, Protein 6.9 g CARB 39g Fibre 2.2 g cholesterol 77mg, IRON 1mg. SODIUM 117 mg, CACL 115 mg
- IT's ok just spend an extra 10 mins at the gym~

220. Lemon And White Chocolate Mousse Parfaits With Strawberrys Recipe

Serving: 8 | Prep: | Cook: | Ready in:

Ingredients

- •5 large egg yolks
- •1/2 cup sugar
- •1/2 cup fresh lemon juice
- •4 teaspoons finely grated lemon peel
- •Pinch of salt
- •1/4 cup plus 2 2/3 cups chilled heavy whipping cream
- •1 3.5-ounce bar high-quality white chocolate (such as Lindt or Perugina), finely chopped
- •5 cups sliced hulled strawberries (about 2 pounds)

Direction

- Whisk egg yolks, sugar, lemon juice, lemon peel, and salt in medium metal bowl to blend. Set bowl over saucepan of simmering water. Whisk until mixture is very thick and thermometer inserted into centre registers 160°F to 170°F, about 6 minutes. Remove bowl from over water. Cool lemon mousse base to room temperature.
- Combine 1/4 cup cream and white chocolate in another medium metal bowl. Set bowl over saucepan of barely simmering water. Stir constantly until chocolate is soft and almost melted. Remove bowl from over water and stir until white chocolate is melted and smooth.

Cool white chocolate mousse base to room temperature.

- Beat remaining 2 2/3 cups cream in large bowl until firm peaks form. Divide whipped cream between both mousse bases, folding in 1 cup at a time (about 3 cups for each).
- Layer scant 1/4 cup lemon mousse in each of 8 parfait glasses or wineglasses; top with 2 tablespoons strawberries. Layer scant 1/4 cup white chocolate mousse over strawberries. Repeat layering 1 more time. DO AHEAD: Can be made 1 day ahead. Cover with plastic wrap and chill. Cover and chill remaining strawberries.
- Spoon strawberries over top of each parfait, if desired, and serve.

221. Mint Caramel Mousse Recipe

Serving: 8 | Prep: | Cook: | Ready in:

Ingredients

- 1 tin caramel treat
- 1oog tennis, or any coconut bscuit, crushed
- 1 slab mint choc
- 250ml fresh cream, whipped
- choc. for decorating

Direction

- Beat caramel treat till smooth
- Add grated choc. And biscuits
- Fold in cream
- Put into glasses
- Top with choc.
- Chill

222. Passion Fruit Mousse Recipe

Serving: 6 | Prep: | Cook: | Ready in:

Ingredients

- 2 cups orley whip(fresh cream should not be used)
- 2 tins condensed milk
- 1 cup passion fruit, with juice and seeds

Direction

- Whip Orley whip till thick
- Add milk and passion fruit
- Pour into glasses and chill
- Decorate with grated milk choc

Index

A
Almond 4,5,49,65,71
Avocado 3,8

B
Banana 3,9
Berry 4,61,67
Biscotti 73
Blackberry 3,11
Blueberry 3,11
Bran 45,46,71
Bread 4,40,41
Butter 3,4,5,12,28,41,46,68,74,88,93

C
Cake 3,4,5,9,10,21,39,41,55,74,89,90,92,93,94
Caramel 4,6,47,108
Cheese 3,4,15,31,32,59,65,70
Cherry 3,4,5,10,15,16,33,65,72
Chilli 76
Chocolate 3,4,5,6,7,8,10,12,15,16,18,19,20,21,22,23,24,25,26,27,28,29,30,31,32,33,34,35,37,38,40,41,42,43,45,46,47,49,50,51,52,53,58,59,60,61,63,64,66,68,69,71,72,73,75,79,80,81,82,83,87,88,89,90,92,93,94,95,96,97,98,99,100,101,102,103,104,106,107
Cinnamon 3,4,5,16,18,67,69,78
Coconut 3,5,33,97
Coffee 3,4,33,63
Cognac 7
Coulis 5,95,100
Cranberry 3,35
Cream 3,4,5,24,32,34,36,38,51,52,59,60,64,80,88,90
Crumble 77
Curacao 14
Custard 4,44

D
Dark chocolate 38

E
Egg 4,44,60,64,65

F
Fat 4,8,14,45,60
Fig 3,30
Flaked almonds 42
Fruit 5,6,73,108

G
Gelatine 4,51,52,60
Gin 4,40,47,54

H
Hazelnut 3,4,6,31,50,51,107
Honey 8,41,67

I
Icing 60

J
Jam 11,37
Jus 7,18,55,81

K
Kirsch 73

L
Lemon 4,6,55,56,57,58,61,67,107
Lime 4,5,53,54,55,59,60,97
Lychee 4,51

M

Mango 3,4,34,59,61,62

Marshmallow 3,4,6,19,65,106

Mascarpone 3,4,7,8,38,55

Meringue 3,20,64

Milk 4,5,63,71,87,89,98,102

Mint 3,4,6,29,45,46,108

N

Nut 4,8,48,49,62,66,70

O

Oil 8

Orange 3,4,5,9,27,62,71

P

Parfait 4,5,6,58,77,85,95,107

Pastry 5,17,67,78

Peach 5,74

Pear 5,74,75

Pecan 3,5,12,75

Peel 23,26,75,90

Pepper 5,23,24,88

Pie 4,61,62,75,78

Pineapple 5,76

Pistachio 5,102

Port 15,16,64

Prune 5,76

Pulse 12

Pumpkin 4,5,42,48,77,78

R

Raspberry 3,4,5,22,26,27,43,80,81,88,89,91,95,99,100,101

Ricotta 3,5,27,82

Rum 3,4,12,67

S

Sponge cake 9

Stew 76,92

Strawberry 3,4,5,6,17,43,59,82,84,85,86,95,107

Sugar 8,14,60

T

Tea 3,29,63

Tequila 5,88

Tofu 5,90

Truffle 3,30

W

Whipping cream 65

Whisky 5,97

Conclusion

Thank you again for downloading this book!

I hope you enjoyed reading about my book!

If you enjoyed this book, please take the time to share your thoughts and post a review on Amazon. It'd be greatly appreciated!

Write me an honest review about the book – I truly value your opinion and thoughts and I will incorporate them into my next book, which is already underway.

Thank you!

If you have any questions, **feel free to contact at:** author@bisquerecipes.com

Jessica Adamson

bisquerecipes.com

Printed in Great Britain
by Amazon